Unshackle
YOUR TEAM

LEARN THE SMART ART
OF BALANCING SALES AND MARKETING!

I0479855

RAGHAVENDRA HUNASGI

INDIA • SINGAPORE • MALAYSIA

Notion Press

No.8, 3rd Cross Street
CIT Colony, Mylapore
Chennai, Tamil Nadu – 600004

First Published by Notion Press 2021
Copyright © Raghavendra Hunasgi 2021
All Rights Reserved.

ISBN 978-1-64951-823-1

I humbly dedicate this book to:

All the marketing and sales professionals around the globe for making business happen.

Contents

Preface

This is your last book on Sales & Marketing

If you Google books on sales and marketing, you will find a few thousand of them and it is ironic today no one book answers all the questions. After reading about a few hundred books, the plan was to write a book that cuts through the noise and talks about how to build successful sales and marketing teams. After being a national best-selling author on Growth, I wanted to take up a challenging task of writing a manual that brings the best practices of both Sales and Marketing. The objective is to help organizations of all sizes, start-ups to enterprises to set up a perfect SMarketing team.

Much of what is contained in this book is a blueprint of how to build successful sales and marketing teams. When you read it you may feel you know it all, but trust me it's worth reading a few times to make sure you implement it all. Knowing it all is generally good, but the key is in implementing what you already know.

This book does not offer quick wins, or 21 days to close a multi-million $$ deal. This book is also not for you if you are looking at a quick fix. This book is the manual that will help you configure a winning sales and marketing team.

In this book, I have tried covering the thought process from the buyer and seller vantage point. I hope this book will help you take your sales and marketing teams to the next level.

– Raghavendra Hunasgi
Your Growth Marketing Zen Master

Acknowledgements

I would first love to thank all the readers of my earlier book *"Unleashing Growth: 15 Growth Marketing Hacks Every Entrepreneur Should Know"* published in 2020 and making it a National and Global bestseller. The recognition gave me the courage to continue my writing and present the best in sales and marketing.

There are thousands of people in the world I am grateful to and the list is never-ending—my parents Praneshachar and Shailaja, my source of inspiration Shruti, Yukta, and Yagna, Dr. G B Rairam and Kiran Rairam for their constant encouragement and support. Dr. Surabhi, Priyanka, and Dr. Ravindra for love and friendship.

Rama Iyer, Kiran T J, Srinivasa Arasada, Ravi Reddy, Srikanth Pakala, Rajesh Jain, Mohit Chitkara, Sairam Vedam, Kalpit Jain, Vineeth Vankara, Ram Kiran Dhulipala, Ramesh Maturu, Sumeer Walia, Rayan Raza and the list goes on.

Last but not least, I would like to thank my editorial team and my publishing lead at Notion Press.

Chapter 1

Welcome to the World of SMarketing

Sales + Marketing =

SMarketing

Introduction

"SMarketing is the new buzzword in the corporate world these days. What is SMarketing, and where has it come from? And why SMarketing and what is its framework? Let us deep-dive into this terminology that denotes both Sales and Marketing."

In the past few years, the term 'SMarketing' has been coined in the industry. The idea was to use the synergy of Sales and Marketing to boost the overall revenue of a business. In the early days of modern business, many companies had separate departments to drive Sales and Marketing functions. They had different structures, leaders, and budgets. The company would treat both departments with entirely different approaches. However, with the staggering impact of continuous disruption, numerous organizations have been left confused, uncertain of how to get a footing in the market. Now, with the recent advancement—SMarketing—the way people do business, a completely new and radical approach has replaced the old rule book.

Definition

SMarketing (sales + marketing) is the terminology used when an organization aligns the goals of the Sales and

Marketing teams to boost overall revenue. SMarketing has become an integral part of the inbound marketing process. Traditionally, the marketing team would transfer qualified leads to the sales team, who then convert the lead to valuable customers.

'For modern organizations working in the B2B market, it is no longer sales against marketing, but a single team—SMarketing.'

As per a research report by the Aberdeen Group in 2010, organizations with proper alignment between the Sales and Marketing teams can achieve a boost of 20% in annual revenue growth. And companies with poor alignment between Sales and Marketing would see a 4% fall in revenue.

Today, many companies have started working harder to create better communication between their Sales and Marketing teams to leverage the true potential of both. It is also fortunate that today, we have access to numerous digital tools to encourage better communication between the two. While improving the bottom-line can be tough, maintaining alignment between these two departments is even tougher.

But in the end, results matter—and this is what every organization works for, day and night. Let us check out the critical framework of SMarketing, which you can develop within the organization to engage and encourage frequent and direct communication between Sales and Marketing.

Framework

First, an organization's Sales and Marketing teams need to be in agreement about the definition of their target group and how they define a business prospect. They should also have explicit knowledge of their respective goals and objectives. What should be the lead generation strategy for the marketing team? How many leads does the marketing team need to generate? What is the timeframe within which the sales team would touch base with the potential lead and the frequency of follow-up after that? Most importantly, the organization needs to ensure that everyone is aligned by simplifying the process.

Whether it is a game of football or business, one plays against an opponent to win—in a game, by the total goals they score and, in a market, by generating higher ROI to maximize profits. To do so, the whole team has to perform together with their best efforts.

Just like football team alignment, aligning your teams is crucial to execute the SMarketing methodology. The Sales and Marketing teams must be aligned along a mutually accepted set of objectives and personas to be on the same page:

Alignment Around a Common Set of Objectives

Defining a standard or related set of objectives and goals for the Sales and Marketing team is the first step. For example, the target for successful or viable marketing pipeline leads could be the same as the sales quota for the organization. Doing this will ensure that both the teams are working towards the same goal in essence and facilitate better communication among the peer network. The idea should be to develop different data-driven communication channels so that the entire team will have clear visibility into the progress that each (Sales and Marketing) team has made.

Another vital step would be to interlink the compensation of both the teams. Doing this would encourage each of the team members to help, support, and push each other to the next level of productivity, which would enhance overall growth.

Alignment Around Personas

Another practice that can be an effective strategy would be communicating about personas to improve the alignment we are talking about. Research and knowledge-sharing among the team members about personas will help each of them to understand the personas better. There could be a specialization of different team members around particular personas, to take this a step further. In the various stages of the funnel, the alignment of the Sales and Marketing team will help them engage customers effectively. Other activities may include:

- Targeting ideal customers/groups
- Engaging with the customers on platforms that they are most active on
- Educating customers by developing various content pieces and activities

Like a football team, companies also want the whole team to work together and bring results to the table. Apart from the different strategies, each player needs to understand all aspects of the game and communicate with the other players and coaches about the strategy, plans, and tactics.

The same applies to companies too. From planning a campaign to successful execution to accounts, everything starts with a conversation between marketing, sales, and other key departments within the organization. Let us simplify this complex framework into simple steps to integrate SMarketing into your organization.

Steps to Integrate SMarketing into Your Organization

- Share the same funnel
- Define lead transfer process
- Open communication with both teams in the same language
- Implement closed-loop reporting between Sales and Marketing
- Implement a Service Level Agreement (SLA), which defines what each team (Sales and Marketing) needs to deliver along with the timeframe

Share the Same Funnel

The top of the Sales and Marketing funnel (TOFU) is the responsibility of the marketing team, while the sales team takes care of the lowest part or bottom of the funnel (BOFU). But what about the middle of the funnel (MOFU)? Yes, there is a middle of the funnel, and it should be the responsibility of both teams.

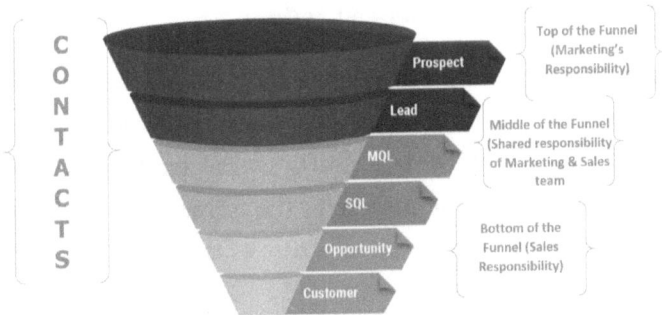

Six Stages of the Marketing and Sales Funnel:

In a marketing and sales funnel, 'contact' is the most generic and essential terminology. At every step, contacts exist, which is very important to both the teams.

Prospect:

Generally, website visitors from different sources, including newsletters, sign-up forms, social media, etc. are prospects. The marketing team is responsible for nurturing prospects to become a lead by creating several campaigns to educate them.

Lead:

When a visitor submits his or her details through a sign-up form or service request form to download an asset like a whitepaper, infographic, guide, or an eBook or get a quote, they are considered a lead. Lead generation is mostly dependent on the awareness of prospects about brands or products or services they are seeking to buy or use.

MQL (Marketing-Qualified Lead):

Contacts who are more deeply engaged with the content, qualify as sales-ready leads. They can be converted to a paying customer by the efforts of the sales team. The MQL stage is in the middle of the funnel, and both the marketing and sales team take care of the MQL.

For example, contacts from a company with a big team (100+ employees) at a nearby location that downloaded a free takeaway from the website would be considered marketing-qualified leads.

SQL (Sales-Qualified Lead):

From the MQL contacts, the leads who qualify for direct follow-up by the sales team (determined by the sales team) are sales-qualified leads (SQL). Once again, this stage is also in the middle of the funnel, and both the Sales and Marketing teams are responsible for it.

Opportunity:

When a member of the sales team has communicated with an opportunity filtered from the SQL at the bottom of the funnel, the opportunity is marked as a legitimate, potential customer.

Customer:

At the bottom of the funnel, finally, an opportunity pays for the product or service, he or she becomes a customer for the organization. Further, they can be retained to purchase the product or service repeatedly; they become a loyal customer.

Daily Communication with Both Team in the Same Language

Regular and effective communication between both the marketing and sales teams—using the same terminology—is essential for them to speak to contacts more effectively, based on the stage of the customer in their journey as a buyer. There must be clarity in the vision for both the teams. The answers to the questions given below from both the teams should be confident and unanimous:

> *'What should be our pitch to a prospect or lead?' or 'What benefit are we offering to a prospect or lead?' or 'At what stage should the sales team take over a lead in the funnel?'*

As discussed earlier, they should understand the targeted persona, different processes of each department, and be in alignment with each other to communicate effectively. They should know each other's functional behaviour accurately, with the goal being complete integration. Daily, weekly, and monthly meetings around the strategies, actions, new launchings, ongoing, upcoming campaigns, etc. will make it simple to achieve this by facilitating open communication.

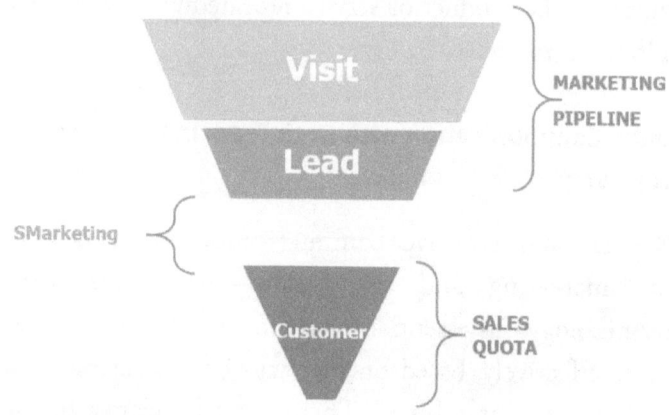

Implement Closed-Loop Reporting Between Sales and Marketing

Reporting is the most critical activity for a team to let the management know about the progress they have made in various activities. But it should be effective, result-oriented, and transparent.

Some of the questions that you need to ask to ensure adequate reporting include:

- Do the marketing and sales team interact, and are they aware of each other's progress?
- Does the marketing team share leads with the sales team? And if they are sharing the leads, what is the quality?
- Does the marketing team have information about the leads they shared with the sales team, including the quality of leads?

- Does the sales team know only contact details, or do they also get content intelligence from the marketing team?
- What is the impact of the marketing and sales team individually and in alignment?

These questions must be identified, which is why you need to implement closed-loop reporting between the two teams. Closed-loop reporting means reporting in a loop that works both ways, allowing more intelligence about the contact to be distributed among the team along with the feedback.

Closed-loop reporting allows:

- The analysis of various lead sources, including organic and paid sources, referrals, etc.
- Proper dissemination of the efforts that the team is putting in and the various activities being carried out to get more leads through different pieces of content

- The measurement of all the time lapses before changing its lifecycle to MQL or final closure of a lead
- To send intelligence along with the contact to the sales team for better conversion
- Communication about the change of lead lifecycle or engagement of lead with website or content and their interest

Implement a Service Level Agreement

While aligning Sales and Marketing teams, a sales-marketing SLA can play a crucial role in supporting both teams to achieve their shared revenue goal(s). SLAs can work both ways:

Marketing Sales

Number and quality of leads to achieve the company's revenue goals.

Sales Marketing

Communication, speed, and follow-ups that help close most of the deals.

The Impact of Digital Transformation on Sales and Marketing

With digital transformation, the buyer's journey has radically changed throughout, and the results have been impressive. Sudden developments in the past few years and the exponential growth of disruptive innovation are fundamentally changing the way of business. Companies and brand managers are working towards digital transformation as they recognize it as the key to innovation, growth, discovery, and creation of new business opportunities.

Lead generation, customer acquisition, and customer retention, along with customer experience, have become the make or break factors in organizations. Since there is a lot of content about products and services available online, customers have become savvy and educated about them. They do not necessarily need to speak to the sales team until they have already decided to purchase.

How Does Digital Transformation Impact the Relationship between the Marketing and Sales Team?

As discussed earlier, digital information has pushed both departments to work in collaboration. The marketing team generates leads via several campaigns, which would then be handed over to the sales team, which converts them to paying customers.

Often, the sales team can reject the leads generated by the marketing team due to quality. They would feel that the leads were not qualified enough to follow-up.

As a result, in many instances, the marketing team can feel disappointed as their efforts to generate leads are being wasted as the sales team would (quite rightly) prefer to focus more of their time on upselling and cross-selling with 'hotter' existing customers.

In such a situation, the marketing team can feel isolated from the customers as they are pushing out marketing messages to them without feedback. Hopefully, digital transformation can change this and improve the relationship between the marketing and sales teams.

Some of the ways digital transformation can impact include:

- Typically, marketing activities are based on gut instinct. Marketers may not be aware of how many leads they can generate and what the return on investment would be. But with digital support, they have an overview of what is happening and depend on guesswork. With the detailed insights they can get, they can remove negative or less productive activities

- Marketers can broaden the scope of what they can do and improve due to access to detailed and real-time insights. This information can not only change the way a marketer treats a customer and brand perception, but it can also enhance consumer experience and improve the immediacy of the experience that they can deliver to customers. What is more, it has changed the way campaigns are created as marketers can now understand the impact of context in a better way

- The way marketing has changed today, marketers can leverage the available data and analytics at different stages of the funnel instead of depending on intelligent guesswork

- For the sales team, they have better data and information access. They can get to work on a collaborative sales technique for better conversion

- Over time, the development in analytics has helped sales, by providing enough information about the consumer's behaviour as the conversion happens right in front of the sales team. Digital transformation offers information access to everyone, affects decisions positively and helps the sales team to be more productive

- Machine-learning services are evolving, which means you can study various patterns to predict the sales and help boost the growth with available data

Additionally, both teams must also understand the precise role of the other. The sales team and marketing team must support each other through the sales funnel. Their functions are specific as listed here:

The Role of a Marketing Team in SMarketing

The main goal of the marketing team is to first create a good impression of the brand in the market. Moreover, they need to generate the reach of the brand and position the brand on top in the perception of potential customers.

Apart from that, here are the roles listed for the marketing team in SMarketing:

- Develop marketing terminology for the rest of the organization
- Own, create, and direct strategies for content marketing
- Engage with customers with great content that will leave a deep impression on the targeted market
- Use all forms of marketing medium and platforms and keep an eye out for upcoming platforms
- Study the market behaviour on several parameters

- Collect user data, insights, study trends, and analyze users' preferences
- Develop a product or service distribution system with various channels
- Execute marketing strategies to achieve the goals of the department as well as the organization's goals
- Analyze the results coming from multiple campaigns

Roles of a Sales Team in SMarketing

The sales department is the one that fuels revenue into the organization. The team requires well-trained individuals with excellent communication skills to interact effectively with potential buyers.

Here is a list of roles of a sales team in SMarketing:

- Work closely with the marketing team to drive sales
- Search for sales opportunities with existing and potential customers
- Detail the benefits of products or services to customers and prospects
- Develop a rapport with new and existing segments
- Understand customers' needs and meet them with the company's current products or services

- Listen to customers' needs and get back to the R&D department with ideas for new products or services
- Maintain relationships with existing clients or customers and develop relationships with potential customers or prospects
- Analyzing sales results and provide feedback to marketing, management, and the rest of the teams

Wrapping Up

In SMarketing, after identifying and understanding each other's roles, both teams can discuss their strategies and collaborate for a win-win situation.

In many instances, the marketing team and sales team can face several problems. Many times, marketing campaigns claim up-and-coming features or offers. However, sometimes, during the sales process, the promised features or offers could be unavailable, leading to bad customer experience. Both teams need to collaborate at each stage. Ultimately, the best customer experience matters and these two teams have to keep this in mind.

Another essential consideration for the Sales and Marketing team in a business is the use of valid data. The absence of correct and updated data can reduce the power of the integration of the Sales and Marketing team. It is essential to root all decisions, actions and plan implementation on a viable foundation of accurate and updated information.

Nothing can beat an integrated Sales and Marketing team. When both Sales and Marketing work in tandem, they can enhance the performance of both the teams. For an organization, it is easier to understand consumer behaviour, their selection process, and decision-making criteria for a product or service when Sales and Marketing work together. Lastly, you require an open, competent and honest communication for effective SMarketing. As earlier discussed, both Sales and Marketing teams need to communicate effectively in a two-way process of listening and speaking.

For companies, the most effective strategy is to have Sales and Marketing go hand-in-glove. Companies can now understand the needs of each customer in a better way. Moreover, SMarketing can boost revenue growth and enable a faster return on investment.

Chapter 2

Sales Blueprint – The S in SMarketing

How a Successful
Sale is Made…

What is a Successful Sale?

"The ultimate success of a sale is when a customer is enthusiastic about repurchasing products or services from the seller, and they will evangelize for the seller by providing testimonials and referrals."

What is Sales—Refining the Definition

The process of selling a product or service is first and foremost a transaction between the seller and the buyer or prospective buyers (the target market), where money (or something of monetary value) is exchanged for goods or services. So, it may be inferred that an excellent way to sell is to focus on the sales skills that are important to make the transaction happen. During a sales negotiation, the seller tries to convince or 'sell' the prospective buyer on the benefits of their offer. If the prospect wishes to strike a deal, they will provide the seller with the agreed-upon amount in exchange for the product or service. Put simply; selling can be defined as the art of closing the deal.

Let us further refine the definition of selling as there can be a massive difference in the sales process, depending on the nature of the product/service. For instance, a necessary sale transaction like buying fuel for your vehicle and buying a car. Majorly, the selling methodology depends on the need for a product or service.

In the first instance, the exchange of fuel is built on a regular and straightforward need and does not need too many details for the transaction to take place. The car's fuel tank is empty, and you need to fill it with fuel. During this transaction, there may not be even a single salesperson involved in any way.

In the second instance, the exchange is grounded on demand for a 'want,' which can be the luxury of owning the car. A car is not something a customer buys frequently. When you think about a vehicle purchase, then a salesperson comes into the picture to inform, advise, and support you with the information to decide to purchase.

Hence, **'sales'** is a broad spectrum where, in most instances, 'selling' consists of the art of coaxing the consumer to buy the product or service and educate him or her about the benefits of the purchase.

A few individuals are exceptionally good at directing and coaxing; these are the super-skilled people who are suitable for sales. You can even say that they are worth their weight in gold.

Sales – Art or Science?

In the business world, it is a common belief that it takes an amalgamation of both art and science for a salesperson to be successful. They need to have a balance of both an inborn ability and a systemic organization. However, there is management science to bridge the tangible and intangible.

Remember the basics, whatever product or service you are selling or going to sell; you need to focus mainly on communicating the benefits of the product or service to the consumer. These benefits may be tangible or intangible, but unless the individual consumer is convinced that the product or service will add some value to his/her needs and they will experience the benefits, the product or service will not sell.

Think, why do women streak colour on their eyelids? Did any person need a fidget spinner or a hula hoop ever in the whole world? It all comes down to the art of selling.

From the Basics of Sales to the Art and Science of Selling

What Makes a Sale Successful?

- **The ability of a salesperson to build long-term relationships with customers:** Good salespeople look for long-term benefits and the opportunity to leverage the current sale into more business in future from the same customer or via referrals, seeking positive publicity via word-of-mouth. (This is a priceless advertisement that you cannot buy!).

The ability of the salesperson to listen and help meet the needs of the customer: Many salespeople spend a lot of their time trying to sell their product or service to the prospective customer, without exploring what the customer wants.

Maybe the customer is not interested in the product you are selling, but he/she may require another product or service that you can sell now or in the coming days. Being an active listener is essential for a good salesperson.

- **Overpromising is a sin when you are selling:** You can lose your potential customer because nothing turns off a customer faster than broken sales promises. This is true of any relationship.

- **Persistence:** It may take several attempts to close a deal successfully. A good salesperson knows this and never gives up on a potential customer until the deal gets closed.

In many circumstances, an email or a phone call reminder might help close the deal, depending on the nature of the product or service, or the urgency of the requirement, etc. A good salesperson is persistent and knows where to draw the line between pursuing a potential sale and annoying the customer.

- **Regular new opportunities and freshness:** Earlier, we talked about the integration of the marketing team with the sales team. To make a successful sale, the marketing team needs to be in the picture, along with the sales team regularly. You need regular emails, website updates, social media postings, etc., so that you can keep customers up-to-date with the latest product or service offerings. Doing this will help the sales team get new opportunities with current customers with updated products or services.

- **Investing in social groups or communities:** We take a lot from society, and it is our moral responsibility to give back to the community you live in by donating to charities, sponsoring community groups, and engaging in volunteer activities. These activities are not only good for society, but it is suitable for businesses as well. Giving back to the community can keep you in the limelight, and this, in turn, increases the likelihood that customers will seek your business when they need your products or services.

An ultimately successful sale is when a customer is enthusiastic about the purchase of products or services from the seller, and this can result in a repeat purchase. In such a situation, a satisfied or impressed customer will evangelize your product or service with testimonials and referrals. Too often, businesses settle for much less than they deserve, and the reason is simple; 'it is the way they sell to the customers'. Let us dive into the sales lifecycle to understand the sales success puzzle more clearly.

The Sale Life Cycle

Irrespective of the product or service your business is selling, almost every sale follows a similar pattern. Ask yourself, what are the steps generally salespeople go through to close a deal? This is the sales cycle. Breaking it into simple steps, the process can be demystified, which helps the salespeople to identify roadblocks and the points to concentrate their efforts.

It is a buyer's journey from the time they realize their need for a product or service to the time of the final purchase. Mastering each of the stages in the buyer's journey is essential to succeed in sales. If a salesperson is weak in any of the stages, they might survive as a salesperson, but they will not thrive. A salesperson can be chronically weak in one or more areas. They need to identify their weak points and keep working on them to improve their sales.

Usually, the sales life cycle comprises of five-seven stages. These are Prospecting, Preparation, Approach, Presentation, Handling Objections, Closing, and Repeat sales plus Follow-up. Let us discuss each of them in brief:

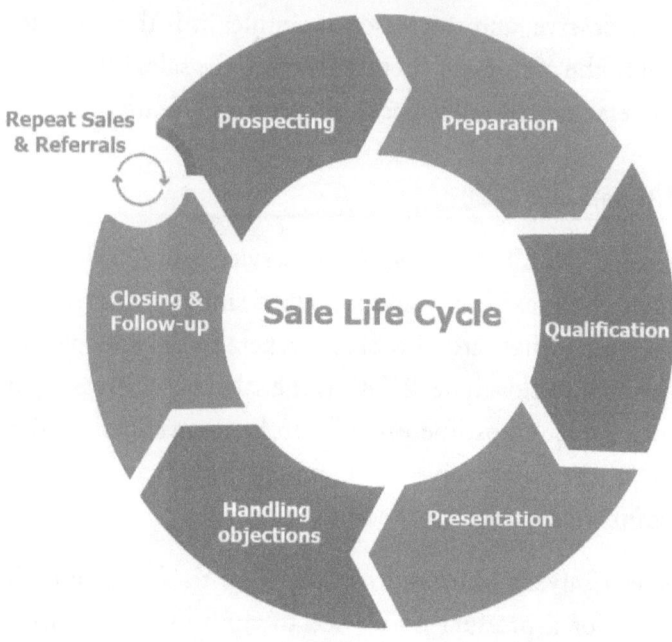

1. **The prospecting stage:** Prospecting refers to the process of exploring new potential clients. Based on the organization, a salesperson might get a list of leads to work with, or they may have to find leads on their own. When you take up the SMarketing approach, the marketing team is responsible for providing leads to the sales team, as discussed in the first chapter.

2. **The preparation stage:** In this stage, the sales team uses the leads collected in the first stage of the sales lifecycle to set up face-to-face appointments rather than try to sell over the phone. Many salespeople prefer to call, but you

can also send emails, use social media, or even mail out sales letters to fix an appointment.

3. **The qualification stage:** Typically, the qualification of lead takes place at the appointment stage itself, although the salesperson can also qualify leads during the initial contact. Majorly, the purpose is to confirm that the lead is both capable and potentially willing to purchase the product or service before the salesperson spends a lot of time trying to pitch to him or her.

4. **The presentation stage:** If you can present your product or service well, you can sell well. In every sales lifecycle, presentation is the core, and it is probably where a salesperson invests the most preparation time. You can improve your presentation with inputs from the marketing team as they have been nurturing the lead through their buyer's journey.

While presenting in front of a client as a salesperson, you need to realize that you are not just selling the product or service, but you are also selling yourself as a trustworthy person. You are representing your organization and its credibility, so your whole personality is essential; this includes your appearance, your body language, communication skills, and more.

5. **The handling objections stage:** At this stage of the sales lifecycle, you, as a salesperson, need to deal with the prospect's concerns. When you look at it practically, objections can be a good sign because they mean that the prospect is at least considering buying the product or service.

6. **The closing stage and follow-up:** After you have made your presentation, cleared the prospect's doubts, and addressed their objections, it is time to ask for a commitment from your prospect. As per reports, this is the second-most ignored stage of the sales cycle, which is terrible given that it is the most important because even highly qualified prospects will rarely close the deal until you approach and request them to do so. An apt analogy for a situation like this is when you ask your guest if they are hungry, but do not serve them food even they have confirmed that they are hungry. As a salesperson, you need to follow-up and close the deal without fail.

7. **The repeat sales and referral stage:** After a successful sale, many salespeople do not give much importance to this stage of the sales lifecycle. Many salespeople are so relieved after closing the sale that they grab their things and race out through the door as soon as possible in the fear that the prospect may change his or her mind. As a salesperson, you need to spend a few minutes after closing the sale, share them their visiting card, and ask for referrals. No sales technique will work better than the referral—many direct selling companies run on this theory. Staying in touch with the customer and maintaining healthy communication after a successful sale can also help you get good referrals in the long-run.

The Team

A successful, engaged, and motivated sales team is gold and does not happen by coincidence; they are forged by an amalgamation of valuable traits shared across the entire team. Every organization dreams of creating a team of sales superstars who will elevate their business to the next level. Below are the traits a good salesperson should possess to make a superstar sales team in the organization:

- **Energetic, enthusiastic, and charismatic:** The sales team should radiate energy, enthusiasm, and charisma, whether they are alone or in a group.

These qualities are infectious and will create an impact on their relationship with customers.

A salesperson without energy, enthusiasm, and charisma can often appear cold, inauthentic, and untrustworthy leading to a lazy team with no results at all.

- **Engaging and interactive:** An organization's backbone is the revenue generated from its customers. A successful sales team would build long-term relationships with the customers, to get future sales and referrals. Engaging and interacting with customers frequently is critical to overall success.

- **Communicative and collaborative:** Good communication skills are the primary requirement in a salesperson. A good salesperson is the one who communicates with the team and collaborates with them whenever required. This builds team rapport, and also ensures that if everyone is on the same page, has the right subject knowledge, and the latest inputs needed to do their job.

Collaboration between salespersons within the sales team and with the marketing team is very crucial for organizational success.

- **Lifelong learner:** Continuous learning is an essential requirement for a successful sales team. They need to thrive in environments where they can learn regularly and are encouraged to seek knowledge. This skill enables a salesperson to be prepared to solve customers' problems.

   Effective sales teams always need to stay up-to-date with comprehensive product knowledge skills, and read educational resources to be an expert in their domain, so that they are at the top of their game.

- **A go-getter with a structured goal:** Every successful sales team must be full of go-getters with structured, transparent, and measurable goals. These goals need to be assessed and measured regularly, and if required, they can be tweaked as needed. A great sales professional always loves challenges and welcome them.

To make a successful sale, a sales team needs to have the above traits, but that alone is not enough. They also need to collaborate with the marketing team as well at different stages of the sales funnel. Let us discuss marketing collaterals here.

Great Marketing Collaterals

Marketing collaterals are a compilation of different media types that are used to help improve the sales of a product or service. Earlier, marketing collateral was majorly associated with brochures, which were used to support the sales process.

But now, companies utilize marketing collateral to inform their targeted market segment informed about their products or service. Today, the term marketing collateral refers to both offline and online media types:

Online Marketing Collateral

The Website

In today's internet era, an appealing, user-friendly responsive website is the primary need of any company. Surprisingly, even today, many businesses do not have decent websites.

The sales team can always use the company's website to showcase the features, benefits, and other required details about the company, its products or services, to prospects. Nowadays, companies enable the lead generation and closing activities through their website.

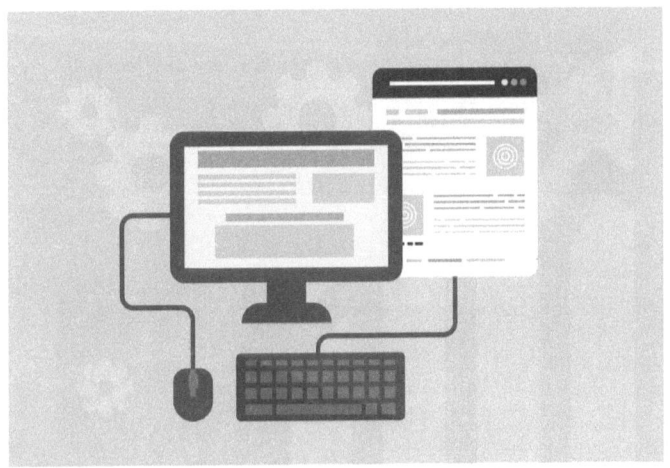

Blogs

A blog can be a useful tool to provide prospects with a lot of information. Blog posts are an excellent way to inform and educate prospects by describing products or services or related topics in detail. It is an effective way to showcase your understanding of your customers' problems and the means you have to solve them. You can also use blogs to tackle topics that are not directly related to your product or service but can be tied back to your expertise. Blogs are an excellent method to nurture traffic into leads and getting in touch with prospects in a non-sales way. It is a good idea not to make direct sales pitches on your blogs.

NOV 10, 2018 / 2 COMMENTS

Car alternatives in modern cities

Lorem ipsum dolor sit amet, consectetur adipiscing elit.
Mauris accumsan enim nisi, sed ultricies neque sagittis sed.
Nam porttitor nisl et enim ultrices tincidunt. Sed sodales
magna ut consequat interdum. Duis ac porttitor massa.
Maecenas et nunc purus. Mauris vel...

NOV 05, 2018 / POST A COMMENT

Interesting places that are not crowded

Aliquam mollis magna tristique nibh posuere, eget
malesuada turpis suscipit. Aliquam pharetra lorem vel nulla
porta, et semper massa posuere. Nullam sit amet luctus
odio. Phasellus sed consectetur dolor. In vulputate ultrices
dapibus. Maecenas dolor odio, malesuada in felis a,...

NOV 01, 2018 / POST A COMMENT

Winter is ending and places are there

Case studies

Companies can use case studies to show prospects about what other customers have achieved in the past by using their product or service. For example, if you are selling a digital marketing tool, you could illustrate how a customer increased his or her ROI by 240% using your device.

Improving Sales Using Web Analytics

Company profile

People want to know about the company and the people behind the organization before doing business with them as they are comfortable entering into business with people they know. The company profile can be used to inform prospects about what makes them tick and details about its background.

Our Company

DESCRIBE YOUR COMPANY

This is a sample text. Insert your desired text here. This is a sample text. Insert your desired text here. This is a sample text. Insert your desired text here.

This is a sample text. Insert your desired text here. This is a sample text. Insert your desired text here.

Let them know about your mission, vision, the year you founded the company, and probably a story behind the business. Other things to show in the company profile include the progress made by the company to date, important milestones, and how the company has evolved so far. Take them through all the essential information via the profile to enable potential clients to learn about the company.

eBooks and Downloadable Guides

In today's digital era, eBooks and downloadable guides are the hottest marketing collaterals. The idea is to provide a free guide or book in exchange for contact details of the prospect to generate leads.

These are PDF files that contain actionable, educational, detailed, and useful information.

Explainer Videos

People spend more than 500 million hours on YouTube to watch videos. Videos are in trend these days.

You can create explainer videos to present the product or service quickly and intuitively to engage with the user.

Videos work for complex products or services, too, and simplify the product's functionality.

Other online marketing collaterals are landing pages, list of partners or vendors, newsletter, portfolio, press releases, whitepapers, etc. which are used by the SMarketing team to enhance the sales process of the organization.

Offline Marketing Collateral

Brochures

Brochures are the physical copy of details about a company or business printed with visual elements to make them appealing. Make sure it is well-designed and provides information about the business, the product, or services in detail to create a positive mind to viewers and prospects.

You can use brochures when you need physical marketing collateral. You can efficiently distribute to prospects without incurring too much expense. It can be easily printed anywhere in thousands for significant events without hampering the budget.

Business Cards

Business cards are an essential tool for every professional to share contact details with external businesspeople. They allow business professionals to swap contact information quickly in a speedy manner.

Calendars and Customized Gifts

In the offline world, calendars are excellent marketing collateral for businesses. People need calendars, and they are happy to get a free one. It is a great way to reinforce the brand to them daily through the calendar, all year long.

Of course, companies use other merchandise, such as pens or cups, for branding with their details engraved.

Other offline marketing collaterals are company/product/ service factsheets, branded envelopes, flyers, point-of-sale displays, company folders, etc. to promote their brands to boost sales.

The Strategy Required for a Successful Sale

Earlier, we have discussed the alignment of the Sales and Marketing team for a better approach; SMarketing. Let us see what happens if Sales and Marketing are misaligned.

In an organization, the Sales and Marketing team will play their role; with no coordination, the marketing team will create a campaign targeting some random group of customers, whereas the sales team will make a cold call or email (provided they have a legitimate interest) to a different group of customers.

Prospects will get irritated, and they will be less likely to respond positively to cold calls or sales emails, if they have not heard of them earlier, and this can negatively impact brand reputation and the chances of closing the deal at a later stage.

Hence, Sales and Marketing teams need to do differently with a 'marketing first' strategy. This means that the marketing team first finds and targets the potential market with a specific problem related to their product or service and show them how it can be solved.

It starts with the marketing team, who warm up and nurture the targeted market by sharing information, educating them on the product or services, and selling the features with benefits.

After that, when the lead is fully aware, educated, and ready to decide on the product or service, the sales team can come into the picture to reinforce the feedback of the marketing team and close the deal. Here, the marketing team should be strong enough to attract the targeted market and convert them into quality leads for the sales team.

Chapter 3

Intelligent Marketing – The Second Half

Data-Driven
Marketing…

Intelligent Marketing

"Marketing processes have achieved a new height as the present leading marketers are starting to fuse AI and ML into their marketing strategies and business plans to make more grounded, enduring client connections."

Intelligent marketing is a data-driven marketing strategy in which marketers use customer interest-based information for optimal and targeted marketing campaigns. This is one of the most transformational changes that have happened in digital marketing in the past few years.

Today, with the availability of a wide range of marketing tools, to record a relevant range of data at any specific stage of marketing campaigns, untargeted broadcasting to mass people has become an outdated strategy. The digital era provides a chance to widen the reach, but with pinpoint targeting accuracy.

With the increase in quality and quantity of user data, other creative and technological developments have evolved with time. As a result, you can see developments in Artificial Intelligence, Machine Learning, Marketing Automation, and more.

Data-driven decision-making is providing answers to questions like who, when, where, what message, and making those answers actionable.

The usage and activation of data, often in an automated or semi-automated manner, allows for a significantly more optimized media and creative strategy. This people-first marketing strategy is more personalized. It has also been responsible for driving considerable ROIs for marketers.

How Can the Marketing Team Accelerate the Sales Cycle?

Sluggish sales cycles can be a source of significant frustration for the marketers as well as the sales team. Fortuitously, there are many steps, which a marketer can take to grease the skids, so to speak, and speed up the sales process.

The key to transforming the sales funnel into a 'slipstream' is to utilize a broad range of marketing methods and strategies to precisely identify targets and supply them with the right information.

Lead Qualification by Marketing Team

Lead qualification is critical to help you focus your marketing and sales efforts on the leads most likely to purchase. Top-quality content is also critical, to capture their interest and retain it as you lead them through your funnel. Transparent pricing helps buyers qualify your solution for their budgets and reach out only if there is a fit. By pre-qualifying buyers this way, you can ensure that only high-quality leads get through to your inside-sales team.

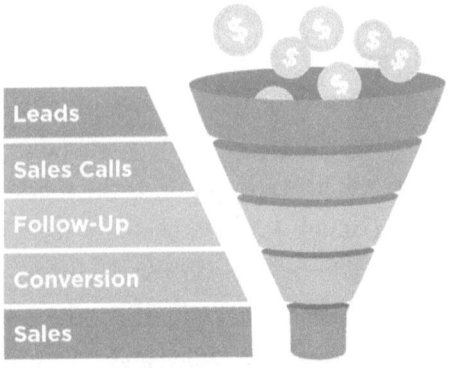

On average, inside-sales cycles are significantly shorter than field sales. To achieve shorter sales cycles, you need leads to make their purchase decisions quickly. Transparent pricing can help your sales team by ensuring that they do not need to spend much time on pricing; instead, they can concentrate on explaining the benefits and features of your solution for a requirement of your target. If this can be done efficiently and effectively, sales conversion can be accelerated. As a marketer, you can make this happen by adopting transparent pricing, and ease the buyer's decision-making process, thus supporting the inside-sales team.

Leads Quota for Marketing Team

The major role of the marketing team is to generate leads, which are transferred to the sales team. The performance of the sales team is a function of the leads received from the marketing team. The higher the number of leads, the more the chances of conversion by the sales team.

Thus, for higher conversion and better sales, the inside-sales team needs a continuous flow of qualified leads delivered at a regular pace. That is why the marketing team must have their leads quota. If the marketing team fails to deliver enough leads to the sales team even for a single month, it will be difficult for the inside-sales team to meet its sales target. This will affect the bottom-line, the alignment between the Sales and Marketing teams, and their morale.

To be successful, the Sales and Marketing teams must work in alignment and define what qualifies a lead as a viable one. Once Sales and Marketing agree on some standard qualifications that define a qualified lead, the marketing team can be held responsible for meeting their quota of agreed-upon monthly leads.

Flexible Campaigns by Marketing Team

Before inside-sales, typically, marketing campaigns had a longer lead-time and did not get effective results until months later. Thus, marketing leaders would plan for a longer marketing cycle; for example, they would start the plan in November, and they would wait until March-April to check if the initial campaigns had worked (or not). Access to data was minimal, and whatever information you did get would often take months to come in.

When you compare the marketing of early days with today's marketing campaigns, you will observe two significant changes:

Marketing campaigns generate more data: When you launch a new marketing campaign through PPC (pay-per-click) ads or social media, you are likely to get lots of user data that the campaign will generate. This data can be used by the inside-sales team to sell the product or service. Earlier, due to a lack of data, this was not possible with traditional marketing methods.

Inside-sales teams generate results faster: Once the marketing campaign starts and leads start flowing in, a competent inside-sales team can close them quickly, within days. You need to be thankful for these shorter inside-sales cycles; even the marketing team can get continuous feedback on the leads and campaign's effectiveness to update their approach and strategy continually.

In this scenario, the only way to succeed is by running agile campaigns that can accommodate feedback from inside-sales. Your inside-sales representatives should be in constant touch with marketing, telling them exactly what works and what does not. Marketing, in turn, should consistently use this data to optimize campaigns for the best results.

Branding

Branding is a critical marketing practice, which can help boost the sales of a company. With the right branding efforts, a company can create a name, symbol, or design that is effortlessly distinguishable as being associated with the company. This helps identify a product or service and distinguish it from other products and services. Branding is vital because not only does it make a notable impression on consumers, but it also lets your customers and clients understand what to expect from your company. It is a way of distinguishing yourself from the competition and building an image that shows prospective customers that what you offer is the better choice for them. Your brand is the depiction of who you are as a business, and how you wish to be perceived.

Some areas help build up a brand, including advertising, promotional merchandise, reputation, customer service, and logo. All of these elements work together to create one unique and (hopefully) attention-grabbing professional profile.

Why Is Branding Important?

Branding is absolutely critical to a business because of the overall impact on your company's image. Branding can change how people perceive your brand; it can drive new business and increase brand awareness.

Branding Helps Get Recognition

The essential reason branding is vital to a business is that it is how you recognize a company and identify with what it offers. The logo is the most crucial element of branding, as it is essentially the face of the company. Therefore, a professional logo design should be compelling and memorable, leaving an impression on a person at first glance. Printed promotional products can be a way to get this impression across.

Branding Increases Business Value

Branding is essential when you try to generate business, and a strongly established brand can increase the value of a business by providing the company more leverage in the industry. This makes it a more appealing investment opportunity because it has a firmly established place in the marketplace.

Branding Generates New Customers

A good brand will find it easier to drum up a referral business. Strong and positive branding generally means there is a good impression of the company among consumers, and they are likely to do business with you because of the familiarity and assumed dependability of a name they can trust. Once a brand has been well-established, word-of-mouth will be the company's best and most effective advertising technique.

Improves Employee Pride and Satisfaction

When an employee works for a strongly branded company that truly stands behind the brand, they will be more satisfied with their job and have a higher degree of pride in the work they do. Working for a brand that is reputable and held in high regard among the public makes working for that company more enjoyable and fulfilling. You can offer quality branded merchandise to your employees. This, along with strong branding elements in your office, can improve employee satisfaction and help create a sense of belonging.

Creates Trust Within the Marketplace

A professional appearance and well-strategized branding will help the company build trust with stakeholders, potential clients, and customers. People are more likely to do business with a company that has a polished and professional image. Proper branding can help you establish yourself as industry experts and make the public feel they can trust your company, the products and services it offers, and the way it handles its business.

Branding Supports Advertising

Advertising is another component of branding; advertising strategies will directly reflect the brand and its desired portrayal. Advertising techniques such as the use of promotional products from trusted companies such as 'Outstanding Branding' make it easy to create a cohesive and appealing advertising strategy that ties in with your branding goals.

Positioning

Positioning is an integral part of the marketing strategy. It aims to position a brand in a certain way, relative to competing brands, in the mind of the customer. Companies apply this strategy by emphasizing the differentiating features of their brand (what it is, what it does, how, etc.) or try to create a suitable image (inexpensive or premium, utilitarian or luxurious, entry-level or high-end, etc.) through advertising. Think your strategy for brand positioning through before you go ahead with it because once you position your brand, it is challenging to reposition it without destroying your brand's credibility. This is also called product positioning.

A proper positioning makes a product unique due to which users perceive a distinct benefit from using the product.

Often, product positioning is also called a USP (Unique Selling Proposition). In a marketplace cluttered with lots of products and brands offering similar benefits, a proper positioning makes a brand or product stand out from the rest. As a result, the positioning can help you distinguish the product, change the pricing as per the perceived image, and still stay ahead of the competition.

When you position your product right, you will find it easier to ride out bad times. Proper positioning is also one that allows flexibility to the brand or product in extensions, changes, distribution, and advertising.

Market Research

"Market research is a critical tool to help companies understand what consumers want, develop products that consumers will use, and maintain a competitive advantage over other companies in their industry."

Market research is the process that companies use to determine the viability of a new service or product via research conducted directly with potential customers. Market research helps a company discover the target market and get opinions, inputs, and feedback from consumers about their interest in the product or service.

The marketing team conducts market research and uses the collected data to develop products and determine how to position the product or service. It also accelerates the sales process with different inputs. You can research through surveys, product testing, and focus groups. The market research teams usually compensate the subjects with either product samples or a small stipend for their time.

Marketing Automation

Marketing automation is about the automation of marketing processes using software and automation tools. Generally, marketing departments automate repetitive tasks such as email marketing, social media posting, and even ad campaigns—not just for the sake of efficiency, but so that they can personalize the experience for their customers. The technology of marketing automation makes these tasks easier. With automation, the sales team can get precise data, and their conversion is more straightforward.

Inbound Marketing

Inbound Marketing is a technique to attract, engage, and delight people and grow a business that provides value and builds trust. With technological shifts, the inbound methodology adopts a human and helpful approach to business. Inbound is a better way to market, sell, and serve your customers. Because when you adopt a methodology that is good-for-the-customer, it becomes good-for-the-business, and as a result, your company can grow better over the long-term.

The inbound methodology has three stages—attract, engage, and delight. Inbound businesses use the method to build trust, credibility, and momentum. It is about adding value at every stage of the customer's journey with you.

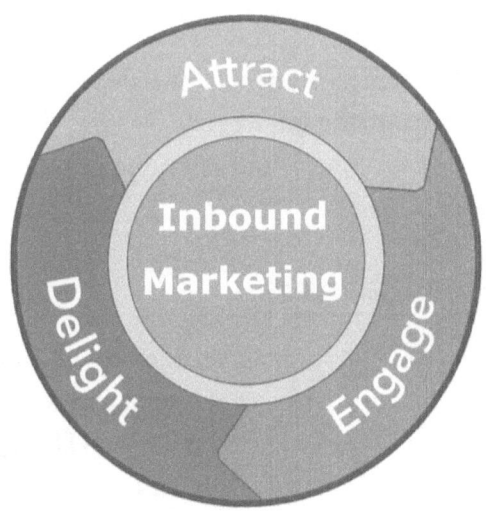

From a business perspective, the inbound methodology represents the growth of your business, and happy customers provide the energy that fuels that growth. Satisfied customers bring newer business either because they buy from you again or because they spread your good name and promoting your product to other people in their network. However, if your customers are unhappy, either to people who are not a good fit for your product or service or because you have overpromised and under-delivered, they will affect your company's growth.

With your teams aligned around an inbound approach, you can provide a holistic experience for anyone who interacts with your business, no matter where they are in their buying journey. To attract customers is not the role of just marketing. In the same way, it is not only the sales team that has to engage customers. And customer delight is not the sole responsibility of the service team. To create relationships that last and customers that stay, every customer-facing team needs to focus on how they can contextually attract, engage, and delight your prospects and customers and continue to build trust in your brand.

Account-Based Marketing

According to Wikipedia, account-based marketing (ABM), also known as key account marketing, is a strategic approach to business marketing. This approach is based on account awareness in which an organization considers and communicates with individual prospect or customer accounts as markets of one.

Account-based marketing can help companies:

- Increase account relevance
- Engage earlier and higher with deals
- Align marketing activities with account strategies
- Get the best value out of marketing
- Inspire customers with compelling content
- Identify specific contacts, from target companies, within the right market

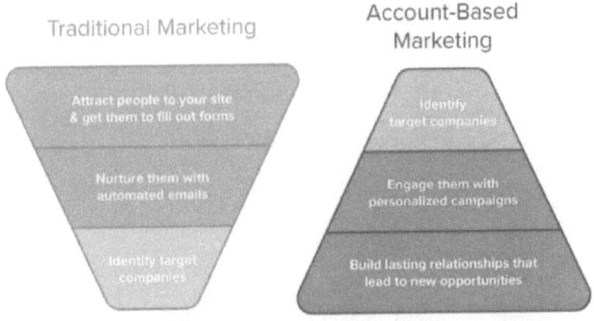

ABM is the best example of SMarketing—the alignment of Sales and Marketing teams. As discussed in earlier chapters, in the SMarketing model, organizations can align strategic marketing efforts with defined sales goals and use feedback from sales to identify new potential markets. For ABM to succeed, mutual working relationship with sales is essential, and marketing needs to measure and optimize their approach based on the accounts they are targeting. ABM targets at accounts (or companies as a whole) as opposed to traditional inbound marketing, which is targeted at leads (or people within these companies). The need for Sales and Marketing alignment also becomes important since there is an inherent disconnect between marketers, who market to people, and salespeople who sell to companies (or structured groups of people).

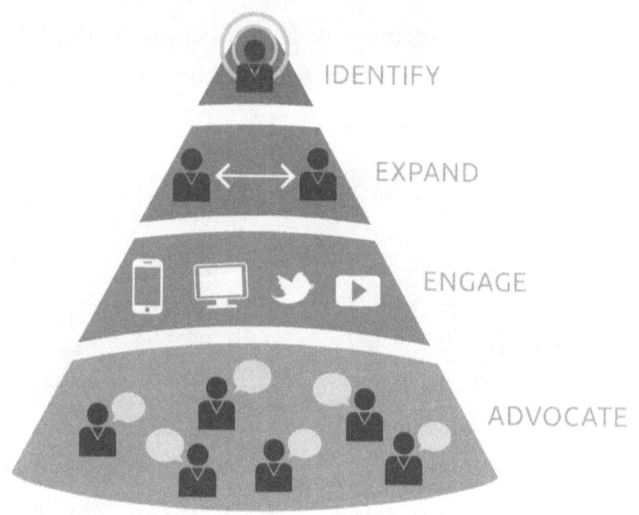

Marketing also needs to take an increased role to develop intelligence on key accounts—as proposed by Peppers and Rogers (1993): "When two marketers are competing for the same customer's business, all other things being equal, the marketer with the greatest scope of information about that particular customer will be the more efficient competitor."

Chapter 4

Hiring a Top-Performing SMarketing Team
– The Team

Framework, Hiring, and Retention

SMarketing Team

"The SMarketing team—is a new breed in the world of business. It is a contraction of the Sales and Marketing team. It is the alignment of your Sales and Marketing teams created through frequent and direct communication between the two."

In the first chapter, we discussed the basics, definition, framework, and took a sneak-peek at SMarketing. In that chapter, we offered you an overview of SMarketing team; now, let us discuss what the SMarketing team looks like—the roles of people and how we can hire and retain them.

Since the end goal (profitability, market leadership, innovative, etc.) of most organizations is the same, it is crucial to integrate Sales and Marketing processes to meet these goals. When you create this team with care, it can make the process of acquiring leads and converting them into paying customers, smoother. What is more, creating the right SMarketing team also helps the customer have a more cohesive experience.

A disjointed experience between Sales and Marketing can lead to confusion for the consumer and result in lost opportunities. The Sales and Marketing teams (or the SMarketing team) need to work to ensure that the customers do not feel like they are being tossed around.

Instead of handling Sales and Marketing teams like separate units that compete with each other, a company that takes a unified approach makes them a part of the same team. When you bring together the Sales and Marketing teams together as allies, it will also positively impact a company's bottom-line. Some companies that have combined their Sales and Marketing forces have reported a 20% revenue growth.

So, How Does the SMarketing Team Look Like within a Company?

It Starts With a Framework

To begin with, an organization's Sales and Marketing teams have to be on the same page about their target group and what they consider a viable business prospect. They should also have explicit knowledge of their respective goals and objectives. What should be the lead generation strategy for the marketing team? How many leads should they generate, and how fast should the sales team follow-up with a potential lead, and at what frequency? Most importantly, the organization has to ensure that everyone is aligned, to make the process more straightforward.

Whether it is a game of football or business, one plays to stay ahead of the opponent—in the game by the number of goals scored and in business by generating higher ROI to maximize profits. To do so, the whole team has to perform together by putting in their best efforts.

Just like the alignment of the football team to play cohesively, team alignment is crucial to execute the SMarketing methodology properly. The Sales and Marketing teams must be aligned to a standard set of objectives and personas to ensure that they are on the same page.

Using common terminology

Furthermore, to work within the same framework, a company's Sales and Marketing alignment hinges on using common terminology for the progression of the entire sales funnel. Having set terms and language will not only make the functions and common touchpoints between the departments more transparent, but it will also ease the buying journey and process seamless for the customer. If the sales team is using specific terminology and the marketing team is using another, then there is a risk that the customer is getting unclear and conflicting communications.

Frequent Sales and Marketing Meetings

While it is good to proclaim that your Sales and Marketing teams work together, you have to work to facilitate it to make it a reality. Regular meetings with a defined agenda that offers time for both the teams to present their side can help in the bonding of the Sales and Marketing teams and help them focus on a common end goal. Sales and marketing leaders should also work visibly and cohesively together to establish and reinforce common objectives and then to ensure that the objectives are being met.

The purpose of these meetings should be to track their collective progress and hone the SMarketing process. Bringing ideas, resources, and suggestions together in meetings can bolster the entire process. Bringing the teams together face-to-face as allies reduces any antagonism, replacing it with the opportunity to exchange ideas and inputs, and build on each other's success instead.

Create Boundaries

Even though the purpose of SMarketing is to bring the Sales and Marketing teams together, there must still be a clear delineation between their respective responsibilities. Clear boundaries must be set to showcase where marketing ends and sales begins so that intrusions can be avoided. After all, Sales and Marketing are two different specialties that require different skills. Employees must know what their particular roles are in a company and how they fit together to keep friction to a minimum.

Closed-loop Reporting

Team members from sales or marketing should be able to tell where a particular lead is in the Sales and Marketing process. They should never be left wondering: "Hey! Whatever happened to that guy I met at that seminar in June?" They should be able to open up a programme and see exactly where that guy is in the buying process. Business 2 Community recommends using both marketing automation software and CRM software to provide data access for both teams and build transparency.

Closed-loop reporting also offers more opportunities for two-way discussions and inputs between the Sales and Marketing teams. They can check in with each other to enhance the process or give each additional valuable customer insights. Aligning Sales and Marketing processes makes both sides feel they're working towards a collective goal.

Creating a sales-marketing alignment plan can boost a company's bottom-line by creating an opportunity to build each other up rather than tearing each other down. Environments, where the Sales and Marketing teams are competitive rivals, do not make much sense when the main objective is the same.

To create Sales and Marketing alignment, a company needs to improve the relationship and conversation between the departments. SMarketing puts Sales and Marketing on the same team for the benefit of the company as a whole. Now, let us discuss how we can hire a smart team.

Hire a Smart Team

We had mentioned before that companies with optimum alignment between their Sales and Marketing teams achieve 20% annual revenue growth in a year. To promote this growth, you must create a stable and lasting partnership between the two teams with a strategic approach that treats them as a single, revenue-generating organization, not competitors. This team within the organization is called the SMarketing team.

To generate the maximum ROI out of your SMarketing team and improve your company's profitability, make sure you hire the right mix of talent.

A typical SMarketing team must be a group of smart and dedicated Sales and Marketing professionals who are qualified and experienced to implement modern marketing techniques with sales ability. The team members must have an inner passion for contributing their part to achieve the set organizational goals of the company.

Manager: Though putting together a perfect SMarketing team is not a tough task; the process must be flawless. The head of the team must be the manager or CEO himself. No matter what the title of the person is, she or he must be aware of the different functions that constitute the SMarketing theme, principles, and professional ethics of the company. He or she must be a go-getter and must be an expert at team management. This person must be competent in creating novel marketing ideas and have in-depth knowledge about the marketing activities of competitors.

Assistant Manager: The CEO must have an able assistant, who is well-versed in all the technicalities of the SMarketing processes. The individual must be an achiever and must be technologically qualified as well as experienced. He or she must be aware of the potential power of the various social networks and must be an active member of such groups.

Digital Marketing Team: As digital marketing is an integral part of SMarketing, the team must hold a capable digital squad headed by SEO experts. The entire SEO team must be in sync with its objectives to enhance their digital footprint. You also need to have a team of able web developers, content managers, and writers to collaborate with this digital team.

Sales & Marketing Executives: These individuals will be directly involved in implementing the policies drafted by the top management. The management can set up an effective and cohesive team of marketing executives by using smartly developed training programmes.

Hiring

Recruiting the right personnel is vital to ensure the success of the SMarketing process. You need to focus on the professional qualifications and experience of potential candidates, along with their attitude. Moreover, the members must be smart and must have team spirit.

Once you have the team in place, it is essential to focus on ensuring that they get the right training. It is essential to specify the company objectives to potential candidates during the recruitment process. Ask them questions around their inputs on how they will go about achieving the company objectives during the recruitment process itself. Discussing the company objectives also showcases the company objectives and their role in it if they are selected.

Adapt the strategies listed below to hire a smart SMarketing team that will work together:

Build a Recruiting Agency Within Your Company

Before you jump on to start the hiring process, make sure it is the right time to hire. Finding a great candidate is just the beginning of your work.

The best Sales and Marketing professionals in the world will not be able to make a positive contribution to your company unless you have the capacity to take them on board and train them.

Create a detailed job description: A detailed job description explains how to perform the job and the responsibilities involved. It includes the following information:

Specify job-related tasks

- The product or service your company offers
- Customer profile that the team will have to work with
- The person they will report to
- What their earning potential can be
- The overall team interaction dynamics

The best way to do this is by interviewing and observing your top-performing sales executives. Focus closely on their tasks and daily activities. From there, you will be able to figure out what the job truly entails.

Make sure to include a thorough employment contract to protect both yourself and your prospect when explaining expectations during the hiring process.

Use LinkedIn and job portals to get fresh applications: To hire great SMarketing professionals, you need to select bright minds among the crowd seeking employment. The more you explore, the more chances are that you get people who are the right fit. Try to share the requirement with a job description on all leading platforms, including LinkedIn to receive quality applicants.

Get your current team involved: Referrals are one of the best ways to get good employees. Involve your existing team and ask them for referrals in return for good referral bonuses. They will get good people for you from their network. This can speed up your hiring process to get a trustworthy potential candidate.

Get it Outsourced

It is no secret that the recruiting process is time-consuming and stressful, which is probably why only 22% of companies feel confident in their ability to hire the right people.

Not only must you get to know your candidate and decide if the person fits the role, but you also need to put in work to create a detailed job description and cast a wide net. A poor hire is bad for company morale; it wastes valuable time and it ends up costing you a lot of money.

It is better to retain the services of a professional recruitment firm if you do not have the time or hiring capabilities. They will recruit the right candidates for you and will also help you with replacements if required. If one of the recruits does not work out, you will not have to waste time scrambling to hire and get on board another candidate right away.

Now that you know how to hire your new SMarketing team, let us talk about how to retain the top performers.

Employee Retention—How to Retain Your Best Employees

An African proverb says, "If you want to go fast, go alone; if you want to go far, go together." A company starts with the vision of one person; then other people come along. A start-up can result from one person's idea, but if it has to become a successful business, there have to be others who believe in the same dream and work as a team to bring the vision to reality.

Retaining good members of an organization is a crucial concern in every company. The company invests time, money, and other resources to hire and recruit employees. However, just after the initial years of employment, many of the recruits leave the company and join the competitors. The personnel department has a significant role to play here. The employees must be paid well, trained well, and treated well. Besides, special care must be taken to boost their morale. Individual recognition is the internal crave of all, and personalized attention will pave the way for employee retention. Let us take a look at a few ways to retain good employees for a longer time.

Plan Retention Before Hiring

Replacing an employee is a costly affair; it costs roughly around 20% of an employee's salary. Your HR manager needs to understand that hiring the right talent is crucial. Have a brief discussion with your hiring manager before they hire candidates. They should have a clear idea about the demands of the job, such as experience, values, degree, and skill-set.

Salary and Other Benefits—Employees' Motivation

As per a survey, around 45% of employees quit their job due to a higher salary. This reason was followed by better career opportunities, better after salary benefits, and work location.

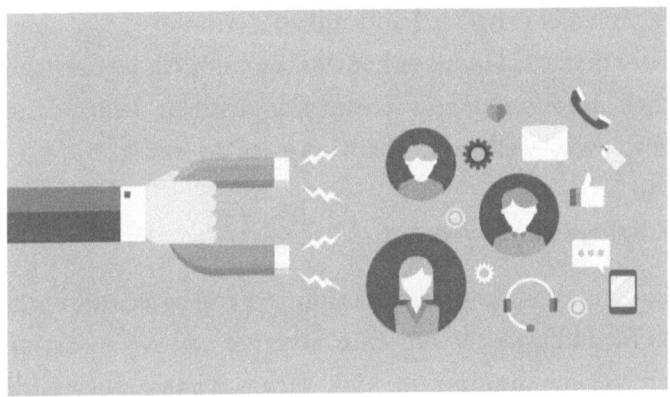

After seeing these insights, you can think why monetary motivating factors such as salary, rewards, including health insurance, EPF, ESI, promotions, etc. are essential. Around 89% of companies use financial incentives to retain their employees. Apart from these benefits, you can take care of the family of your employees by providing several benefits, including medical benefits to their family, holiday trips, etc. This will help your employees to connect with you and your organization emotionally. If you treat them as part of an extended family, they will treat you like a family.

Conducive Work Culture

Are your employees happy to work at the company? Do they look motivated when they come in, or when they leave? They say that employees do not leave the company; they leave the boss. Monitoring team leaders and their behaviour towards their fellow teammates is as important as monitoring the team's profit graph.

A mentally exhausted and unhappy employee can never be as dedicated to his or her work as required. Understand their needs and wants; create a department dedicated to employees' wellness at the workplace if possible.

Employee Engagement

For any organization, retention is a real issue and needs to be addressed, in any case, whether you are a start-up or already running on high turnover rates. Increasing employee engagement can always be helpful to improve retention and also results in better productivity and increased employee satisfaction.

Employee engagement can be achieved by involving employees in the business planning process, knowledge-sharing activities, etc. Since employee engagement is a different topic, we will take that up in another chapter. You can look at employee retention strategies here.

Open-Door Policy

Top management is not easy to access in organizations. Most of the time, people have bitterness against company management, and they do not have an idea of where to raise it. Many of them do not even discuss those issues during the exit interview.

Many a time, employees want to share their view or idea directly with the top management, to get recognized. But they cannot do that due to the interference of middle management.

Now, this is something every organization should consider. They need to create an open-door policy and not just on paper. Nowadays, it is easy to create online fora or query points to allow your employees to shout their hearts out. Also, you need to address those concerns and take suitable actions to avoid dissatisfaction among your employees.

Respect Diversity

Every person has his own pace to learn and perform. Some are slow but steady, and some might prove to be fast-paced. Some take a lot of time but still are not able to deliver quantity but outrun everyone in quality work. However, some can provide work in bulk but with compromised quality.

Every person indeed gets the same training, equal knowledge transfer, and live sessions, but you cannot expect the same outcome from everyone. As soon as you find out what makes a person tick and ignite their energy, the better it would be. Respect this diversity and have faith in your decisions.

ESOPs for Early Employees

Plan for the retention of early and loyal employees by offering them part ownership of your company. Employee ownership can be provided in multiple ways. You can offer them the option to buy stocks of the company directly, provide stock options as a bonus, or make them part of a profit-sharing plan.

When you think of your employees on these lines, they start feeling a sense of ownership, engage better, and work for a longer term. This is a win-win situation for both the organization and employees.

Training and Growth

Individuals join any organization to be able to grow their career, learn, and grow. You can kindle this requirement by training them and sponsoring to attend workshops.

You should enable and encourage them to upgrade themselves in their career by providing them cross-functional training, help them develop new skills, and explore more significant opportunities in the organization.

Let us wrap up this portion by concluding that your employees are not automatons, performing their tasks for a mere paycheck, though that is important too. They are living beings who also care about their workplace, nature of work, people with whom they work, and many other factors. In the SMarketing scenario, it is always essential to keep the above points in mind instead of getting involved in an unbeatable wage bidding war, which could wipe out your bottom-line, most of the time. Your Sales and Marketing teams are the primary building blocks of your business; you need to nurture them if you expect them to nurture your business.

Chapter 5

The Process

How
Marketing Can
Accelerate Sales
Enablement…

The Process

"SMarketing is a fundamental part of the Inbound Marketing methodology. In this process, which is usually implemented in the 'middle' of the sales funnel, the marketing team transfers qualified sales opportunities to the sales team, which then closes the sale."

Earlier, we had discussed the definition of SMarketing, the impact of digital transformation on the Sales and Marketing teams, how the marketing team can accelerate sales, and how to hire a SMarketing team. Now, let us discuss 'the process and how marketing can accelerate sales enablement.'

We have discussed that it is imperative that both teams direct their efforts towards the same objectives to boost the revenue. Unfortunately, this is not always the case. Around 85% of the terms each team uses to describe the other are negative; often, sales teams accuse the marketing team of sending irrelevant or poorly nourished leads, while marketing accuses marketing of not closing their generated leads.

Through SMarketing, inbound marketing aims to get the best from both teams by coordinating their functions and having them work towards the same goals. Marketing and sales must be two halves of the same team and work together towards a shared purpose within the organization. Always remember that innovation is the key to increase business. Let us start the process of SMarketing with the 3Cs, i.e. communication, coordination, and collaboration.

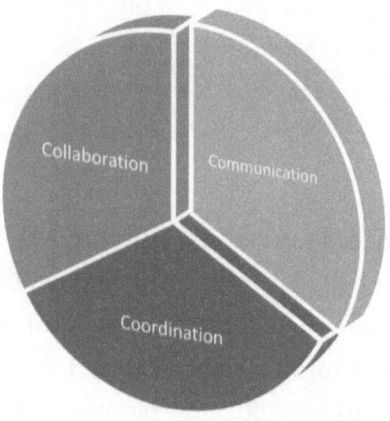

Communication

Start developing a regular and meaningful dialogue between Sales and Marketing workforce

The marketing and sales teams have to communicate regularly to get their jobs done. But to create optimal efficiency, the communication has to be detailed and insightful. Organizations need to have clear definitions of what the sales team is looking for in a lead so that the marketing team can create campaigns accordingly. This can be a solid first step towards stable alignment. If you do not have this yet, then it is a good idea to invite your counterpart to lunch and start the discussion. Bring data to review why some leads were followed up and the reasons why others were not. Look at new customers that went through the pipeline the fastest and keep an eye out for commonalities.

Once you have a common understanding, get it all down in writing so that you have agreed-upon definitions. Then make sure you can track these definitions to different stages and measure conversions from lead-to-sales accepted (sales-qualified leads—SQL) leads. Ideally, you will also have a step in between for marketing-qualified leads (MQL) so that the marketing team can scrub out anything that does not meet the qualifications that the sales team wants before you qualify the leads and add them to the queue for the sales team to take up a process which we have already discussed in earlier chapters.

Coordination

Continually heighten the outcome of Sales and Marketing efforts

After getting clarity on definitions such as SQL or SAL, MQL, etc. it is time to create a feedback loop for continuous improvement. This means getting the Sales and Marketing leadership together frequently to review results and make changes in lead definitions or even campaign spend according to the feedback. Many organizations do this every quarter as 'QBRs' or 'Interlocks.'

No matter what fancy name you give to these meetings, make sure that both departments understand the purpose and what they need to bring to the meeting. These meetings become worthless after 1-2 sessions if it is just the marketing team showing data and asking for feedback from the sales team. BOTH sides need to come with data and be prepared to provide insights and call-outs from the data.

Here is how both teams can do this. Create some dashboard reports that both teams can access for the following data:

- Highest and lowest performing campaigns for the quarter in terms of SQLs, opps, and closed won (six different reports)
- Highest and lowest performing inside-sales reps (or telemarketers) for the quarter in terms of conversions to SQLs, opps and closed won (six different reports)

Both parties should analyze this data before the coordination meeting and come prepared with feedback from their teams on the reasons and insights towards the results. Having the analysis and team input take place before the meeting (from both sides) will make these meetings more successful. As you mature in this process, you may be able to set goals for conversion rates and use that as a bar to analyze what campaigns over or under-performed.

Collaboration

Get significant revenue growth by working towards the common goal

Now that you have excellent communication and you are meeting regularly to obtain coordination, what more could you possibly achieve? The answer is collaboration. At this stage, the lines between the marketing and sales teams start to get fuzzy intentionally.

The marketing team starts doing things that fall in the realm of the sales realm, and the sales team starts getting involved in marketing programmes, otherwise known as SMarketing. With SMarketing, the offices of the VPs of Sales and Marketing would be next to each other, and they might even report to a centralized executive like a chief revenue officer responsible for both marketing and sales.

While this may sound like a scary alternative dimension, when you Start SMarketing, it can be awesome! This stage means the end of the blame game as both the Sales and Marketing teams are genuinely working together to achieve the mutual goal of the company growth. The bonus plans of the marketing team would be based on revenue, not leads. There is mutual respect because these groups are in tight alignment.

How can a company achieve this state of *nirvana*? It is a lot easier than you think. At the heart of SMarketing, collaboration is the Sales and Marketing teams working together on a joint programme. This means designing the programme, promoting it together, and tracking the results together. This is the essence of SMarketing.

The most effective plan to achieve SMarketing collaborative alignment is a referral marketing programme. While the sales team already understands that referrals are their highest quality leads, most sales folks do not often ask enough or have a 'give-get' to offer. With help from marketing and a referral marketing programme, sales can not only get more referrals but turn the referrals into their most productive lead source. Data from the referral marketing programmes running on the referral platforms shows an average conversion from lead to purchase of 35%.

This conversion rate is possible through referral software that enables collaboration between Sales and Marketing by integrating into the sales CRM to allow marketing to create the brand message for the programme and sales to help execute it. This enables marketing to extend its lead generation team to customers or partners who can connect your message to target buyers in their networks.

Bottom-line—this scalable personalized lead generation works so well because both marketing and sales back it.

Craft a Sales and Marketing Agreement (SLA)

Companies that commit to using inbound marketing to grow their business must not only talk the talk about aligning Sales and Marketing, but they must also craft an internal protocol (usually called a Service Level Agreement or SLA) between sales-marketing teams that spells out how they will walk the walk, together.

Creating an SLA is a foundational element of an optimized inbound marketing programme. However, according to HubSpot's annual 'State of Inbound' report, only 25–50% of organizations actually have one.

Talk about a missed opportunity! HubSpot's research shows that companies whose marketing and sales departments are well-aligned see 20% annual revenue growth, while those that do not have an SLA see a 4% decline.

With so much revenue on the line and reports to back it up, you can see how crucial it is to craft and implement a successful SLA. And HubSpot is among those offering a free Service Level Agreement template.

As discussed earlier, *"An SLA is a contract between (Sales and Marketing) departments that aligns goals and outlines agreed-upon expectations. Instead of constantly battling over leads, an SLA holds both teams accountable to specific, measurable goals."*

To sum things up, a well-crafted SLA will align Sales and Marketing using mutually agreed-upon definitions, commitments, procedures, and metrics, as well as vigilant documentation, transparency, and robust communication.

Simple, right?

Not really! Crafting a winning SLA is actually can be quite challenging, yet eminently doable and worth the effort.

The Sales and Marketing departments can work together to put together a mutual agreement that documents:

- What constitutes a marketing-qualified lead (MQL)?
- How many MQLs marketing will generate each month
- How marketing will hand over qualified leads to sales

How Sales Will Handle the Lead From There (Quick Response Is Considered Essential)

Basically, marketing makes a commitment to sales regarding the quantity and quality of leads that the sales team needs to help sales meet their company revenue goals ('We promise to give you lots of great, qualified leads!'), while the sales team agrees to protocols regarding timely, high-quality follow-up, and detailed documentation ('We promise we will contact these awesome leads immediately, with verve and élan!').

Transparency and ongoing communication are essential to this process, and you can augment this by using shared databases and automated systems that allow both sides to track (on customizable dashboards) their progress towards those shared goals in real-time.

For Better Results, Craft a Lead Disposition Process

OK, so now the leads are rolling in. Sales and marketing are more closely aligned than ever before. What if the company is still falling short of reaching revenue goals? Let us assume, for this discussion, that marketing is meeting its commitment to deliver X number of quality leads, etc.

Successful industry practitioners have learned that for the system to work at maximum effectiveness, it is imperative that the sales team adheres to a carefully crafted 'lead disposition' process designed to enforce your companies agreed-upon SMarketing best practices and ensure consistency across the sales force.

The Lead Disposition Process May Include

- Detailed, repeatable protocols (as well as tools such as email and voicemail templates) for making contact with qualified leads

- Coordination with marketing to better understand a particular campaign or product offer and how it might help solve a problem for a potential customer
- Total commitment by sales to document every aspect of the process

"The idea is to apply a consistent set of activities that respond to the prospect's inquiry or behaviour without overwhelming them," according to blogger/author Matt Heinz, president of Washington-based Heinz Marketing. "An effective (lead) disposition process either reaches the prospect for qualifying, disqualifies them as an inappropriate prospect, or hands them back to marketing for ongoing nurturing until they're both qualified and ready to buy."

How Can Marketing Accelerate Sales Enablement?

From the beginning of this book, we have been emphasizing the importance of inbound marketing in the world of business today. It is in sync with the new buyer behaviours. It matches how people shop. It allows you to market your products and services and reach your audiences in the most effective way possible.

But inbound marketing on its own is not enough. It is a great start—but if you have not invested in sales enablement yet, you're missing a vital piece of the puzzle. Inbound marketing and sales enablement work hand in hand, side by side, and you need both to take your business to the next level. Sales enablement will allow you to maximize the results of your inbound marketing.

Sales enablement can give your salespeople the tools and strategies for effective collaboration. It can help them understand what type of information they need to be sharing and what value they can bring to the table. And it will help them realize how they will benefit from their collaborative efforts.

Continue with the Inbound Experience

The inbound experience does not, and cannot, start and end with your marketing team. Your sales team must continue to educate, please, and delight your inbound customers long after marketing has handed the leads off. Customers would not be happy if they were informed, nurtured, and cared for, for half of the buyer's journey, only to be then lied to, cheated, and pressured into a sale afterwards. The inbound experience must be flawless, from start to finish.

With sales enablement, your salespeople will learn how to communicate with inbound leads, how best to reach out, and when to reach out. They will learn what selling tactics to use and which outdated selling techniques to get rid of. They will learn how to offer value and how to delight customers. They will learn to prioritize the customer experience to increase sales.

Your inbound marketing team has worked hard to bring in leads. Do not let your salespeople ruin these sales opportunities. Teach them how to become inbound sellers through sales enablement to ensure that you do not waste the efforts your marketers have put in.

Tools and Technologies

Sales enablement also consists of arming your salespeople with the right tools and technologies. These tools will give them structure, insights, and data intelligence. It will save them time through automatic data entry to capture specific details. It will enhance productivity and help them close deals by assisting them to generate more leads, track behaviours, identify important prospects, and deliver content at the right time and in the right place.

Many of the technologies can also be integrated with your marketing automation software to ensure an efficient flow of information between the two departments to ensure that no data is lost, no miscommunications occur, and everyone has access to the same information and content. These tools will empower your salespeople for the best results.

Step-by-Step Process to Sales Enablement

Getting enablement right is not something you can do in a day and forget about. It requires vision, dedication, and commitment at the highest levels of the organization and coordination throughout the business.

That said, the essential steps to develop an effective sales enablement system are relatively straightforward.

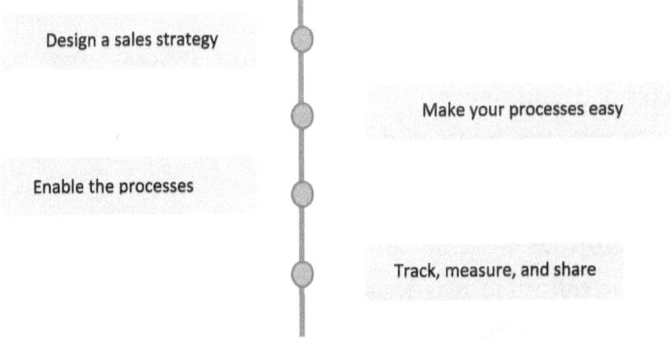

Design a sales strategy

Make your processes easy

Enable the processes

Track, measure, and share

Design a Sales Strategy Aligned with Your Buyers

Almost too obvious to mention, but you need a plan that aligns with your buyers' desired outcomes; you need products or services that positioned and communicated in a way that makes them exciting and appealing. If your sales process is complex, your value propositions need to be more tailored to each prospect, and you need to invest in a more personal touch. In a complex sales environment, HOW you sell becomes critical, and maybe the last differentiator in a world when offerings look the same to buyers. Once your strategy is designed and your offerings well-positioned, your team needs to know HOW to sell most effectively and efficiently, which takes us to our second point:

Make Your Processes Easy to Learn and Follow

Overly complicated sales processes developed at the strategic level, documented in a manual, and then stuck on a shelf are not going to enable your sales force.

In complex B2B sales, an effective process may be complex and dynamic, but that does not mean that you cannot make it easy and fun for your sales team to learn and follow it.

Develop straightforward, customer-focused processes (some call these playbooks) with stages, milestones, and steps. Then embed these processes into the salespersons' workflow so that they are in front of them over their day and guide them to each next step in a dynamic way. The workflow has to start from prospecting to opportunity management, account planning, and customer success.

Enable the Processes with Training and Content

Training that never leaves the classroom is a waste of time and money. Align your training with your sales processes, and then put training materials directly into the hands of salespeople, embedded in the same workflow that guides them through their processes.

They should be able to access training videos and articles at the precise moment when they need them, such as before a customer call, or when dealing with a customer problem. A system that serves up training content precisely at the right points in the process can enable salespeople to practice and perfect new skills at the moment when it is most effective.

Likewise, Sales and Marketing content should be at their fingertips when they need it. If a salesperson has to go digging to find the right piece of collateral or does not even know the content exists, it will not do them much good. Develop a system that puts Sales and Marketing content in front of salespeople directly inside their workflow, exactly when they need it, based on a dynamic set of criteria.

Train Well Again and Again

Managers who only coach at quarterly or annual reviews are not contributing to sales enablement. Train your managers in your sales processes and methodologies and enable them to coach salespeople in a regular cadence, aligned with what each salesperson needs to focus on to reach the next level in their performance.

Develop a dashboard of crucial analytics that includes both lagging and leading indicators and the ability to drill down to better understand each salesperson's performance and the reasons for their performance. Teach managers to use the analytics in tandem with coaching conversations to understand what each salesperson needs and how to help them achieve their goals in a step-by-step, consistent manner.

Track, Analyze, and Share

Collect data and analyze your process against goals to enable constant improvement. Make it easy to update the processes to reflect best practices and new insights based on win/loss analysis and other data.

Let us start this piece by asking how essential sales enablement is for your organization. The reality is that we operate in an increasingly complex and competitive environment. While your organization might survive for a while without a formal sales enablement function as long as you have a few top players on the team, the teams that will succeed in the future are those that figure out how to get their entire orchestra playing expertly together today.

In our opinion, sales enablement is the most critical factor in whether your sales organization will survive and thrive in the coming years.

Chapter 6

Creating a Winning Formula

Best Practices of
SMARKETING…

Best Practices of SMarketing

"When Sales and Marketing teams are aligned to form the SMARKETING team, businesses see around 40% growth in the closing rate. In this chapter, we share the best practices for SMARKETING and the specific tools that you can use to help your organization work together to empower your sales team so that they can close more deals."

Until now, we have been discussing the definition of Smarketing, the impact of digital transformation on the Sales and Marketing team, how a marketing team can accelerate sales, and hiring a Smarketing team. In the fifth chapter, we discussed 'the process and how marketing can accelerate sales.'

Let us dive a little deeper into this concept and discuss some best practices of Smarketing. With the best practices, you will be able to understand how Smarketing is better than traditional Sales and Marketing. With our inputs, you can get started with your strategy as we outline a few Smarketing best practices.

Focus on Smarketing From Top-Down

Achieving complete Smarketing success is a significant commitment and will take some time and effort. The larger your organization, the more of a process it will be, and potentially the more time it is likely to take. Therefore, the initial commitment and passion for this alignment must come from the very top.

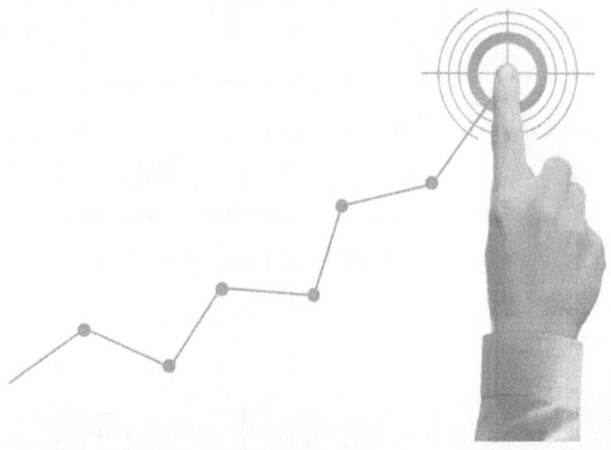

Sales and marketing working in tandem to enable more sales should be a high priority to the CEO. The CEO should take ultimate ownership to ensure progress. Why? You ask. Check out these stats to understand why this is important:

- You can get 200%+ higher revenue from marketing-generated leads
- Win more customers for a longer time—40%+ higher probability that marketing-generated leads will close
- Keep those customers forever—36% higher retention rates
- Around 24% faster three-year revenue growth and 27% faster three-year profit growth for B2B

The next step is to get complete buy-in from the Sales and Marketing leadership, starting from the director-level, middle management, and the entire team. Garnering the right level of commitment to this new concept may involve making a few changes in personnel.

Some companies choose to bring in an additional operational supervising executive who has experience with these types of alignment efforts to help get everyone on the same page. Others may choose to combine their Sales and Marketing under a single executive. No matter how you do it, the important thing is that no matter who an employee goes to within the company, the language, information, and enthusiasm around Smarketing should be the same.

Establish and Track Combined Smarketing Efforts

Key Performance Indicators (KPIs) are quantifiable and trackable means to evaluate the success of a company or department. You can set goals and specific steps towards attainment in advance; the results can be tracked against those agreed-upon metrics.

Typically, KPIs start at the top, with everyone contributing to the overall success of the company. Then, they are divided into each department, which is then distilled down into each individual employee contribution. Sales and marketing are still very different and equally important departments; however, to achieve Smarketing success, you will also need to have a set of joint KPIs. This ensures that both departments are aiming for the same goals, yet have their own contributions to help get there. The agreement of agreed-upon KPIs is called a Service Level Agreement, or SLA.

Typically, Sales and Marketing operate within the sales funnel. An essential Smarketing best practice is to ensure both teams are working within the same funnel with a single, agreed-upon customer journey and unified messaging. The teams could work together to come up with email templates for sales to utilize that are consistent with the content being pumped out by marketing. This allows for a single narrative for your customer, with combined and more consistent resources for your employees.

Time to Get Acquainted

Often, in companies where marketing and sales are misaligned, there tends to be tension that may create an even more significant gap between the departments. You will hear things like, "Marketing sent me this terrible lead, the customer had no idea who we are or why I was calling," or, "I handed over a super-hot lead to sales, but nobody followed up."

The first step to create understanding and remove tension is to get everyone together for them to realize that all of them are on the same team and that they are working to accomplish the same goal—more sales. Both sides are in for their customers and to generate revenue for the company (and themselves). It is good to acknowledge that they are all human and could make mistakes and that they should use the experience to improve their performance.

One of the best ways to break down some walls and allow your Sales and Marketing teams to get to know each other is to host events specifically for them. Some options are to provide a company-hosted happy hour, a combined lunch, or an organized team-building event.

The important thing is to get them together outside of the typical work environment and provide them with a forum to connect, chat casually, and get to know each other. Such events cannot be a one-time effort. You should provide regular, recurring situations that allow your Sales and Marketing teams to spend time together and blow off steam. This not only allows everyone to see each other as people instead of entities but also creates avenues for individuals to build relationships. They are, therefore, even able to develop communication channels between the two departments when they have questions during work hours.

Smarketing Requires Excellent Communication

Another Smarketing best practice is clear and concise communication. The idea here is to disperse the agreement, understanding, language, and effort that management has agreed upon, down to the two departments.

First, host a Smarketing kick-off meeting that will introduce the core idea and concepts around your new strategy. You should cover the reasons you are making this a priority, as well as precisely what it looks like to the company and what it means for each individual contributor.

After this, you need to create simple ways for collaboration and communication between teams. Allow salespeople the ability to share new information they learn from customers. Ensure marketers know how to get a hold of someone in sales when they have a question and vice versa.

Keep sales up-to-date on all marketing campaigns and offers by keeping the marketing calendar visible to everyone in the department. Have marketing provide talking points to the sales team around specific offers or campaigns to help drive home the intended message.

Keeping information flowing freely back and forth between the departments can make both teams more successful, reduce tension, and ensure your customers are their primary focus.

How Smarketing Is Better Than Traditional Sales and Marketing?

Every business needs stellar Sales and Marketing professionals if they want to succeed. However, traditional business models within the IT and professional services sectors have often seen discord arise between the Sales and Marketing functions. A previous school of thought and a lack of communication had these two teams working independently and in many cases with individual priorities, targets, and goals.

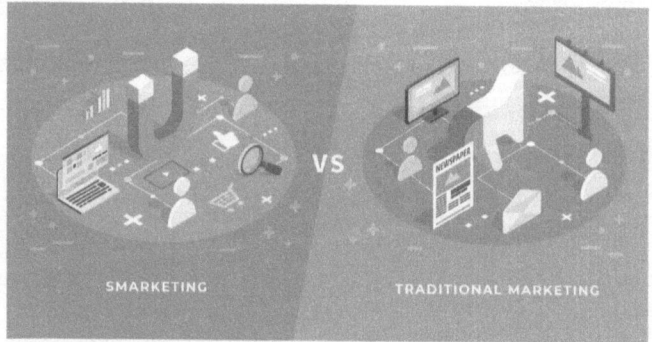

The truth of the matter is that if a business wants to be successful, the Sales and Marketing teams need to work together. If you have read previous chapters, you will know that today's prospects do not rely as heavily on sales teams as they once did; this is because we are in the digital age, and our prospective customers now rely more on digital content for information for their purchase decisions, which is why Smarketing comes into the picture.

The advantages of the unification of Sales and Marketing, otherwise known as 'Smarketing,' is a massive opportunity for B2B organizations to maximize their lead generation and therefore achieve the ultimate goal of increased return on investment.

Smarketing Team Can Provide You With Relevant Resources

Your prospects have discovered you because your business offers a product or service that they require. By the time a prospective customer is ready to be contacted by you and your sales team, they will be further on in their buyer journey and closer to making a purchase. It is at this point that you can turn to the marketing team for blogs, videos, infographics, and other pieces of content that you can send to prospects to help them gain more information about your product or service, and additionally will reassure your prospective customers that your business is ahead of the IT market curve.

A better relationship between the Sales and Marketing teams will also mean that the marketing team can create content that is relevant to the questions your prospects are asking. The sales team will receive the same queries day-in, day-out, so marketing can utilize this and create useful and compelling content such as a blog listing out FAQs or an eBook. Doing this will ensure that prospects can find the answers to their questions much quicker, and you can close a warmer lead.

Smarketing Establishes Credibility

Your marketing team understands how to grab the attention of a prospect and how to hold it. The marketing team can write useful content, create beautiful infographics, eBooks, emails, and much more. High-quality content such as this will create a better brand image, which will help your business credibility. This means that prospects will have more trust in you and your sales team, making the sales process much smoother, overall.

Your marketing team can suggest the best offers based on current industry trends.

Trends can change and evolve almost instantaneously, and perhaps even more so within the IT and technology sectors. It is marketing's job to keep up-to-date with what trends are growing in popularity within the marketplace and which propositions are losing traction.

Early identification of emerging trends can provide sales with the opportunities to take advantage of a shifting market. Successful Smarketing requires your Sales and Marketing teams can work together to find these opportunities and move ahead of the competition.

Smarketing Can Help You Stay Ahead of the Competition

A successful marketing team needs to keep an eye on their own product or service, and another on competitors'. They should be well-versed about the blog posts, social media promotions, and other content offers that your competitors are putting out into the world, and they should relay this back to you and your team.

This means that when a prospect asks your about your product or service compared to your competitor's, you will be able to give a clear and knowledgeable answer and enter into a conversation about why your service is a better fit for them.

An Increase in the Number of Sales Leads Qualified

Marketing will A/B test multiple ideas, with the ultimate goal of generating high volumes of marketing-qualified leads. Some of these campaigns will result in a multitude of marketing-qualified leads and be highly successful from a marketing point of view. But to the sales team, these leads could be much more challenging to convert or realize a much lower sales value.

A good Smarketing relationship will allow the sales team to discuss with marketing how these campaigns went from their point of view. As a result, it means that marketing can focus on effective strategies that prioritize lead quality over quantity, and the sales team can convert more sales-qualified leads, filling the pipeline with successfully closed deals.

It can take time and effort to build a healthy SMarketing relationship, but the rewards are more than worth the time. HubSpot suggests that when Sales and Marketing are aligned and working towards a shared goal, the organization can realize a 20% annual revenue growth, 36% higher customer retention, and 38% higher sales win rates.

SMARKETING – Low-cost and High-return Method

At a high level, calculating the cost of customer acquisition (COCA) is relatively straightforward in the software industry. It is merely the total Sales and Marketing expense for the period divided by the number of customers acquired in the period. Easy.

After the introduction of Smarketing, it has become something of a buzzword in most organizations today. It brings clients to you through the use of mutual efforts of the Sales and Marketing teams. Many of you today must wonder, "What is the ROI of Smarketing?"

ROI is usually much higher when the Smarketing team works, than traditional techniques, including higher-qualified lead generation, increased traffic and sales revenue. The precise figures will depend on how much you invest and how well you utilize Smarketing techniques. Smarketing provides low investment with high-return because of these critical factors:

Customer journey: Some of the steps of the CDJ (customer decision journey) have been switched to the digital world. Initial steps like information gathering and vendor comparison are entirely digital. The experience that Smarketing provides customers is better and different.

Decision-making process: There is a big bunch of people involved, direct or indirect, in the Smarketing team. We can split them into decision-makers and influencers. Each of them will have a vital role to play during the customer's journey, and the information they provide will be from marketing as well as sales perspective.

Buying cycle: Due to the above point, the cycle is shorter and more comfortable. There is no waiting time, unlike traditional methods. With qualified leads, the sales team feels quite comfortable in closing the deals and customers also need lesser time to decide to purchase.

At its heart, marketing-sales alignment is about processes. If you can create clear and goal-oriented procedures that foster a close relationship between both departments, while also effectively distributing tasks and reducing the burden on each, the margin for error is dramatically reduced. What is more, you will be able to save a sizeable chunk of time and money in this process, and so will your customers!

Chapter 7

Developing the SMarketing Culture

Inculcating Values and Methods to Consolidate the Winning

SMarketing Team

Introduction

'You cannot stop after creating a winning formula; you need to embed it in the team's genes. This means a top-down approach where the entire team unabashedly believes in the synergy of marketing and sales to create a winning SMarketing team.'

The winning culture or in this case, the SMarketing culture is not an easy change despite the many benefits it has. This is because it is in the very nature of the marketing and sales team to view each other with a certain rivalry. The marketing team believes that the efforts they put in to get the leads into the pipeline are never appreciated.

And the sales team believes that the efforts they put in to close the deal are nothing short of a Herculean task. However, the SMarketing approach proposes a massive turnabout in the way both the teams think.

In the earlier chapters, we had looked at bringing the leaders of both the team together, setting expectations right, having SLAs in place, and coordinating with each other at every level of the inbound journey. However, that is just the starting point.

'Organizations today are evolving every day to meet the challenges of the market and the needs

of customers. A step forward is working towards a culture where marketing and sales not only work together but also respect the efforts that each puts in to generate revenue.'

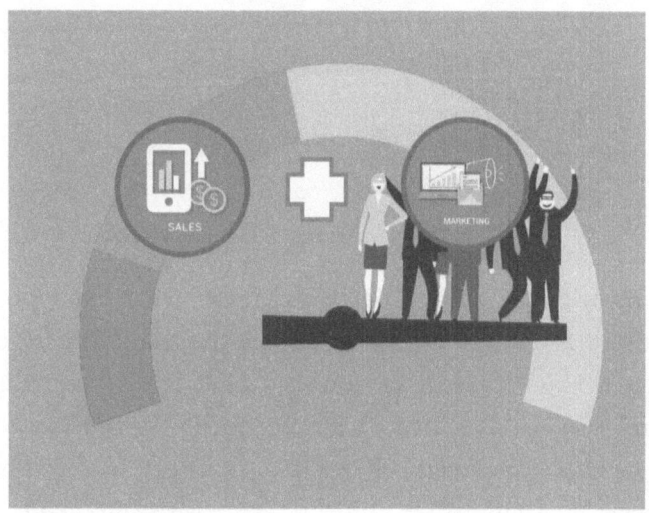

The winning culture

While all companies do undertake some training around marketing and sales for the respective teams, it usually is not enough. The training typically comprises of the products they have, the kind of technology they use, a list of the main competition, the market segmentation, and what the teams are supposed to be working on.

Most training sessions start with an overview of the organization that has the mission and vision statement. While the aim behind sharing the vision and mission statement is to inspire, it rarely does. To the Sales and

Marketing team, it is just a bunch of words that sound pretty.

Here is where you need to take the SMarketing approach. Under the SMarketing approach, the Sales and Marketing teams will not only be guided through the 'what' and 'how' (vision and mission), but also through the 'why' (the purpose) behind what the company does. It is only when the customer-facing teams like the Sales and Marketing, or rather the SMarketing team knows why the company does what it does, will they be able to forge ahead in the right direction.

Arrange for Common Training Programmes

The Sales and Marketing teams have different objectives to fulfil. However, they are heading in the right direction. It is as if their goals are tagged to each other. Here is what the structure of the training programme should look like:

The Story of Why:

We have talked about how the personas and definition of a lead for both the Sales and Marketing teams should be the same. It should go back one more step to make the meaning deeper. This means that both teams need to know why they are doing what they are doing. Defining and firming up the purpose of your business is essential to the continuity of the company.

Make It Simple:

Often companies make the mistake of making their story convoluted and confusing. When they do this, they lose the interest of the teams during the training programme. Breaking down your products or services makes the Sales and Marketing teams included and necessary. They start realizing that the purpose they serve is worthy. It helps them build up confidence in the product or service they are marketing and selling. The most successful marketing and sales teams are the ones who believe in what they are selling. The belief they have in their products and services adds credibility to each of their interactions with their customers.

Help Them Create Value:

Now that you have clarified why they are doing what they are doing and helped them believe in the worthiness of the product or services they are selling, it is time to teach them how to create value. Marketing has to be able to position the brand and the product or service in such a way that it creates the perception of value in the minds of customers. The sales team has to be able to tell customers how they can gain discernible benefit from the product or service in comparison to the competitors. Each piece of content and demonstration that is presented to the customers either directly or through channels has to help create value.

How to Close the Gaps:

Most marketing and sales teams do not produce synergistic value because there are gaps in the way a lead is nurtured through the funnel. During the training programme, you can take the marketing and sales teams through the entire process. Each team can take it in turns to point out the gaps that arise. For instance, the sales team may tell the marketing team that the difference can occur when they are not aware of the content the marketing team has been using to nurture the lead. On the other hand, the marketing team can show the sales team how to keep the marketing team in the loop to ensure that the right content reaches the lead at every stage.

Speak the Same Language:

This point is a follow-up of the above point. It is a formal agreement between the marketing and sales team to agree upon certain aspects of the way they present their products and services. This means that both the marketing and sales teams should talk to the product or service teams to understand the features of what their products or services offered. More importantly, it is even more critical to understand the limitations of the products or services. The features have to be understood in absolute terms, as well as how they fare against the competition. Once the knowledge is gleaned from the product or service team, both the Sales and Marketing teams have to list down the way they will speak the same language at every customer touchpoint.

Walk the Talk:

One of the best ways to learn lessons is to walk a mile in the other person's shoes. While this may not be possible in real life, it is good to do it in a controlled environment. One of the most common problems that the Sales and Marketing teams talk about is how the other does not understand how difficult their job is. In an ideal world, it would be a good idea to switch jobs once in a while, but that may not be possible. However, we can conduct some workshops as part of the training, where the Sales and Marketing teams assume each other's roles. It will allow the teams to become empathetic towards each other's work and move one step further towards becoming a SMarketing team.

Activity and Results:

Human beings thrive on recognition, and that is true of result-oriented activities like marketing and sales. What is more, this has to be an ongoing activity and not just part of the training programme. However, during the training programme, make it a point to outline all the activities that each of the teams would be in charge of and the results that they need to bring in. Use the SMarketing training programme as a forum to set the responsibilities of each team and how the results from one team ties in with the duties of the other. Doing this can be very important as both of the teams need to understand how the work of one feeds the work of the other.

Celebrate Together:

Make the marketing and sales team share numbers that they have worked on till now and celebrate together. As training is going to be an ongoing activity it makes sense to make both the teams aware that they will need to work on SMarketing together to be able to celebrate together.

During the celebration, encourage them to share the details of the journey and evolution. Make it a point to invite the marketing and sales partners (that worked on a lead together) on the stage together. Ask them to show how they interacted and collaborated on several touchpoints to make a successful sale. Create case studies and best practices from all the experiences that the teams have had in collaborating.

Make Them Accountable:

While working together and learning from each other is crucial, it is equally important for each of the teams to understand what they are responsible for on their own. It is imperative to end the training session with clear duties for each team along with the areas in which they are supposed to support each other. Ensure that all present understand that the underlying responsibility is to generate more revenue, build a good reputation, and consolidate their market share.

Does Size Matter?

What is the ideal size of a marketing team? Does the sales team have to be bigger, equal to, or smaller than the marketing team? Why does the size of the team matter? As everyone knows, the size of the team has a direct impact on the cost of marketing and sales as you have to compensate each team member in terms of salary and the bonus on the leads they have generated and the deals they have closed.

Have too big a team, the costs go up, and the results may not be comparable with the results they have produced. And if the team is too small, there is a likelihood that they may become overworked and not provide the kind of attention they need to give to each customer. In such circumstances, the team may become jaded and tend to become demotivated. The idea is to build up a team that works like a well-oiled machine that generates leads and converts them to deals.

One-on-one Team Coordination:

In some companies, they team up a marketing person with one salesperson. This has the advantage of ensuring that both marketing and sales have perfect coordination. The results, however, depend on the calibre and attitude the marketing and salespersons bring to their work. Even if one person lacks the aggression and inclination to work it can create an unbalanced outlook and result in reduced sales all around.

TEAMdynamics

Domain or Area-wise Division:

In some instances, the company goes by the domains or areas that a marketing person is responsible for. This marketing person or team works with a sales team that is responsible for the same domains or regions. Depending on the domain or speciality you are dealing with, you can determine the size of the marketing and sales team. When you go with a team approach, then ensure that the mix in both teams is that of less experienced and matured people. As a result, you can see that you have a balance of a calm and knowledgeable outlook, along with the freshness of innovative ideas. However, one of the points you have to keep in mind, for any team type you form does not become too inter-dependent.

Independent Sales and Marketing Team:

With this approach, the marketing team and sales team will not have to focus on a particular domain or in coordination with one partner but focus on marketing the brand and company as a whole. In the same way, the sales team will also have to take an aggressive and dynamic approach to the leads they will work on to convert into successful deals. While this approach can create some amount of conflict and confusion in the way the marketing and sales teams work, it can also result in better results. However, you need to ensure that both the teams are mature and focus only on the growth of the company and not just on the individual growth, though that is also important.

How to overcome SMarketing bottlenecks

No matter how much training you provide your SMarketing teams, reorganize your teams, and incentivize them, there are bound to be bottlenecks in your journey to becoming a successful SMarketing team. However, not all conflict is harmful and often it can be a symptom of something more profound. The more you know the root of your problem, the easier it will be to solve. The first aspect of SMarketing that you have to understand is that it is not a formula that you apply once and expect results forever.

The very concept of SMarketing is all about being dynamic and preparing to face all the challenges of today's competitive digital market with an integrated strategy. Which means that you need to strengthen the roots of the sales-marketing coordination. Unless you can get the basics right, there is not much use in going ahead with the SMarketing concept and approach.

Get Your SMarketing Right

Your SMarketing approach will only work when you have the strategy down pat. And please note, the strategy has to be dynamic, which means frequent evaluations and revisions to suit the changed circumstances. We give here some of the steps that you can take to ensure that the strategy is right and bottlenecks are minimized.

Budget for the Best Fit:

The SMarketing budget has to be put together, keeping in mind the results you expect. While the budget is not the only factor that contributes to your SMarketing success, it does play a huge role. Sit together with the SMarketing team to decide on what you hope to achieve in the immediate future and the long-term. Then work backwards on the efforts you need to make to achieve the results. When you do that, you will be clear on your pay-per-click advertisements for short-term results and the SEO (search engine optimization) efforts for organic growth in the long-term. The budget aspect needs to be time-bound and you will need to keep looking at the results that you have produced with your SMarketing efforts to tweak it accordingly.

Update Customer Profile And Persona:

While most companies in the B2C (business-to-customer) and B2B (business-to-business) sector have a typical customer profile and persona in mind when they start selling their products and services, it would be prudent to revisit this profile and persona regularly.

Why? Because the market is evolving all the time, which means that the profile of the customer also keeps changing. What is considered a luxury today may become a necessity in the future. Take a car for instance. In the yesteryears, only the higher income class would consider buying one. But in recent times the purchase of a car has become an aspirational goal for the middle class and even the lower class. It is an excellent idea to do some market research on the profile and persona of your customers.

Plot Your Customer's Buyer Journey With Care:

Your customer goes through a complete thought process and a detailed journey before deciding to purchase. The buyer's journey would vary a lot based on the product and the sector as well as the cost of purchase and the value of the product or the service to the buyer. At each stage of the journey, the buyer may go through some thought processes and would undertake some steps (like checking testimonials, referrals, social media, comparison, etc.) before moving along the next level. Only with the knowledge of the journey that a potential buyer undertakes can you build the right kind of SMarketing support required.

Both the Sales and Marketing team needs to speak the same language and make the right moves to ensure that the customer has all the information he or she needs to move along in the right direction. You would be surprised to learn that many companies have not updated their customer's journey to the purchase decision.

List Out What Makes You Different:

What is your product or service differentiator? Can your SMarketing team answer this question objectively? Are they aware of what your competitor offers and how your product or service measures up against their offer? Do you know the pricing structure that the market expects? Can you explain why a customer should be willing to pay your price?

Do you have a proper comparison of your product or service measures up against the competition? If your customer asks for it, can you provide a ready-to-use comparison sheet? One of the ways you can create credibility and market leadership is by being a helpful authority in your field of work. To do that, you need to be clear about your product or service differentiator.

Focus on the Marketing Collateral:

Marketing collateral is any piece of content that you use as part of your SMarketing efforts. This not only includes your blogs, articles, thought leadership, whitepapers, case studies, testimonials, nurture emails, but also includes your videos, images, infographics, social media posts, etc.

As you know, your marketing collateral plays a vital role in the buyers' journey by providing them with the inputs they require to make a purchase decision. In the earlier steps, we have talked about how you need to revisit the customers' profile and persona, their buying journey, and the product or service differentiators. The logical next step is to update your marketing collateral according to your findings during the update of the customer persona, the differentiator, and the buyer's journey. It is crucial to ensure that all your marketing collateral has a distinct style, voice, and tone. Make sure that you brief your creative teams about the way you wish to be perceived by your website visitors, leads, customers, and the world on the whole.

Improve your website and online assets

In the virtual world, your website plays the role of your storefront and needs to play a vital role in all your

SMarketing efforts. Even as you are working towards our marketing collateral in conjunction with the way you see your customer personas, it is essential to start working on improving your website. Your online assets will be playing a massive role in the way your customers see the value your company can deliver. The site and online assets make a promise of what you can offer and provide a preview of how your customers will benefit from buying your product or service.

The experience they have on your website and the information that your online assets provide need to be seamless. Every promise you make in your headlines and taglines has to be delivered by the pages and the online assets. View the whole package from a third-party point of view. Be objective in the way the experience has panned out for you. If you feel that your internal team cannot do a fair job of evaluating the website and your online assets, it is better to invest in a third party agency who will do this for you. Give due importance to SEO (search engine optimization) so that Google will show your website in related keyword searches. Doing this is not an easy process and cannot happen overnight. But promising and delivering value in terms of your website and overall messaging can help you do this.

Evaluate and Formalize Your Sales Process:

Salespeople by their very nature are dynamic and have a unique approach to the way they deal with customers.

Most salespeople jealously guard their techniques and keep sharpening it based on their success rate. Some salespeople tend to have a flexible approach where they make the customer feel that they are feeble and use this approach to draw out the customer's needs before putting forth their offer. Some salespeople go full-on and take the aggressive approach. They overwhelm the customer with their sales pitch but do it with charm and style.

While sales style is a personal and unique approach, the process for sales should be uniform and organized. It is essential to talk to the whole SMarketing team and come up with a process that everyone can follow. Ensure that each person in the team has a chance to look at each of the steps to validate them to see if they are still relevant and then formalize the process. You would be surprised at the number of steps that have been finalized in the past and have lost their relevance in today's world.

If possible, take the teams through a mock trial of how a sales call works out and then finalize the steps that will remain a part of the sales process.

Write Down the SMarketing Strategy:

SMarketing is a synergy where the Sales and Marketing teams come together to work in collaboration with each other to produce results that are exponentially better. To do this, you need to not only evaluate every step of the process, formalize processes but also come up with the SMarketing strategy. However, it has often been seen that while strategies are discussed and finalized, they are rarely implemented. This could be because the team has gotten too busy with the mundane and routine everyday tasks. Do not let that happen with your SMarketing strategy.

What you need to do is write down the strategy so that you can all read back what has been decided and reflect on that. Reiterating the main points and highlights of the strategy at the start of every SMarketing team can also work to keep the strategy on the top of the mind of the entire team. Doing so is vital because you do not merely come up with a strategy but actually implement it.

Keep Track of the Progress and Plan Tactics:

No SMarketing plan will ever take off unless you have a list of key result areas based on all the analyses you have done and the strategy you have put in place. One of the ways to do this is to look at the conversion rate of the sales team and work backwards to the number of leads that the marketing team needs to provide. Unless we have the parameters on which you will evaluate, have both teams called out explicitly and have them accept it.

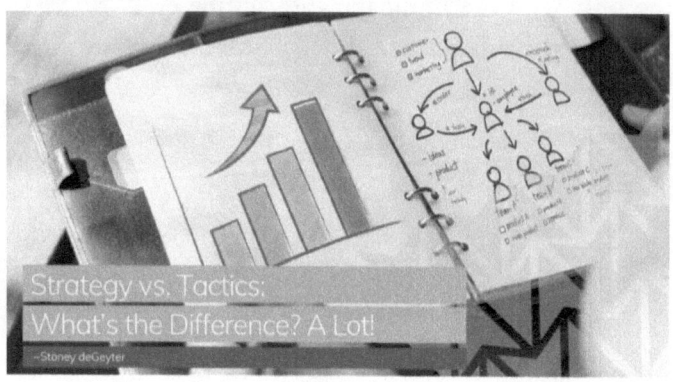

Strategy vs. Tactics: What's the Difference? A Lot!
~Stoney deGeyter

But that is just the first step. You will need to break down each of the key result areas and define the KPI or key performance indicators. Then you need to work backwards to come up with tactics to make sure that the team is empowered to achieve them.

Draw timelines for each of the activities and ensure that everyone responsible knows what they are supposed to do and by when they will be required to complete it. Lay down the sequence in which the completion of one activity by one team starts the other on their activity. Ensure that you have the service level agreements in place. Even with this level of detail, you will find that there can still be a gap in the way the Sales and Marketing teams work.

You will need to make meaningful interactions between the teams on a friendly but competitive level, a regular occurrence. Have the leaders of both teams commit to being a part of this interaction. Any way of thinking and working that you want to inculcate in your organization has to flow from the top-down. That is the only way, you will be able to ensure that the SMarketing attitude is part of the teams' DNA.

Wrapping Up

Bringing about the SMarketing culture is not a one-time thing but a way of thinking that will make numerous changes at the very heart of your company's culture. In the process, you may even be forced to make some harsh decisions to ensure that you have pruned the SMarketing team to have nothing but the best of talent.

Chapter 8

SMarketing—It is Just the Beginning…

How to Achieve SMarketing Success!

Summary

"No longer is SMarketing a choice but a necessity in today's cutthroat competitive world. SMarketing is the best way forward for companies on their inbound marketing journey. It is all about the synergy that Sales and Marketing can bring together rather than as separate entities."

In this chapter, we will look at the journey of discovery that we went through in the past few chapters.

In the first chapter, we introduced the concept of SMarketing, where we defined how Sales and Marketing can help each other in the sales process. Then we looked at the framework where we talked about the following:

- Alignment around a common set of objectives
- Alignment around buyer personas

After this, the next steps would include:

- o Sharing the same funnel
- o Define the lead transfer process
- o Encourage open communication between the teams
- o Implement close-looped reporting between Sales and Marketing

- o Put in place a Service Level Agreement between the two teams
- Sales and marketing to share the same funnel

We also looked at the six stages of the marketing and sales funnel:

- Prospect: These are visitors to the website from various sources
- Leads: When the visitor offers his or her details to download some information
- Marketing-qualified lead: When the lead engages well with the content shared, then he or she would be considered an MQL or marketing-qualified lead
- Sales-qualified lead: When the sales team also qualifies the lead as a viable one, then it is called a sales-qualified lead or sales-accepted lead

- Opportunity: The definition changes to opportunity when the sales team has communicated with the lead and found them to be viable
- Customer: When the lead purchases the service or product or signs on the dotted line of the contract, he or she would be considered a customer

Furthermore, we examined the impact of digital transformation on SMarketing and how it helps customers have an enriching buyer journey and increases sales. We also clearly defined the changes that will happen to the role of the marketing and sales teams in SMarketing.

The second chapter was about detailing out the sales blueprint, as the S in SMarketing stands for sales.

We looked at the definition of a successful sale where a salesperson is able to identify the need of a prospective customer and then enable him or her to understand that their product or service will meet their need.

We also tried to define if sales is an art or science. The conclusion is that there are definite elements of science and art in the process.

The anatomy of a successful salesperson would include the following:

- His or her ability to connect with a customer and maintain a long-term relationship

- The ability to listen and understand the needs of a customer and help them buy the product that will meet their need
- Learn to refrain from overpromising to get a short-term sale and then lose the customer in the long-term
- Be persistent without irritating the customer and offering helpful inputs

The SMarketing team will need to help the sales along with the following:

- Keep the marketing efforts fresh and generate new opportunities
- Invest in social groups and communities to improve the company's image

Sales cycle defined:

- The prospecting stage
- The preparation stage
- The qualification stage

- The presentation stage
- The handling objections stage
- The closing stage
- The follow-up stage
- The repeat sale and referral stage

Here is a word portrait of how the team would look like:

- Energetic, enthusiastic, and charming
- Engaging and interactive
- Communicative and collaborative
- Lifelong learner
- A go-getter with structured goals

We also outlined what we meant by marketing collaterals:

Online:

- The company website
- Blogs and articles
- Case studies and testimonials
- Company profile
- EBooks and guides that can be downloaded
- Explainer videos

Offline:

- Brochures
- Business cards
- Calendars and other giveaways

All these marketing collateral need to be whetted by the entire SMarketing team to ensure that they can answer questions, provide information, and engage prospective customers.

The second half of SMarketing is intelligent marketing, which should be data-driven. In today's digital world, marketing needs to be savvy and ensure that they use all the technology at their disposal.

We also defined the steps that the marketing team should take to quicken the cycle:

- Lead qualification by the marketing team
- Define the leads quota for the marketing team to fulfil

- Flexible campaigns for the marketing team so that:
  - o Campaigns will generate more data
  - o The inside-sales team can produce results faster
- Concentrate on branding because:
  - o Branding builds recognition
  - o It increases business value
  - o It generates new customers
  - o Improves employee pride
  - o Creates trust in the marketplace
  - o Branding complements advertising
- Concentrate on branding
- Undertake market research
- Marketing automation is important

Have an inbound marketing engine that can attract, engage, and delight customers through the buyers' journey. We also defined how account-based marketing is another aspect that can help you with:

- Increase account relevance
- Engage earlier and higher with deals
- Align marketing activities with account strategies
- Get the best value out of marketing
- Inspire customers with compelling content
- Identify specific contacts, from target companies, within the right market

In the fourth chapter, we looked at the guidelines to hire the right SMarketing team. We also went deeper to define the framework for hiring and retention.

- It starts with a framework definition
- Get the team to use standard terminology
- Have frequent Sales and Marketing meetings
- Create Sales and Marketing boundaries
- Have closed-loop reporting

Here is how the SMarketing hierarchy would look like:

- Manager at the head to create flawless strategies
- Assistant manager to manage the next steps
- Digital marketing team with SEO at the centre
- Sales and marketing executives to set things in motion

We also looked at how to build a recruitment agency within the company:

1. Get the job description right
2. Specify job-related tasks

3. Use social media and job sites to get more applications
4. Get your team involved

Have an employee retention plan in place:

- Plan retention even before you hire
- Motivate employees with salary and benefits
- Create a conducive work culture
- Employee engagement is important
- Have an open-door policy
- Respect diversity
- Offer ESOP to early employees
- Promote training and growth

In the next chapter, we looked at the process of SMarketing where marketing would accelerate sales enablement. SMarketing is based on communication, coordination, and collaboration.

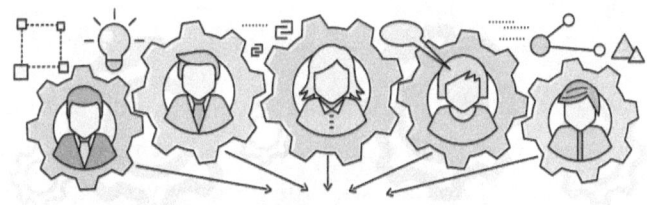

- Communication: Start developing a regular and meaningful dialogue between Sales and Marketing workforce
- Coordination: Continually heighten the outcome of Sales and Marketing efforts

- Collaboration: Get significant revenue growth by working towards the common goal

We also talked about the process to craft an SLA (Service Level Agreement) between the Sales and Marketing teams.

The Sales and Marketing departments can work together to put together a mutual agreement that documents:

- What constitutes a marketing-qualified lead (MQL)?
- How many MQLs marketing will generate each month
- How marketing will hand over qualified leads to sales
- How sales will handle the lead from there (quick response is considered essential)

Craft a lead disposition process for better results:

The lead disposition process may include:

- Detailed, repeatable protocols (as well as tools such as email and voicemail templates) for making contact with qualified leads
- Coordination with marketing to better understand a particular campaign or product offer and how it might help solve a problem for a potential customer
- Total commitment by sales to document every aspect of the process

The next step is to look at how marketing can accelerate sales enablement:

- Continue with a productive and useful inbound experience
- Leverage tools and technologies to add value to the process

Here are some more steps to follow:

- Design a sales strategy aligned with your buyers
- Make your processes easy to learn and follow
- Enable the processes with training and content
- Train well and keep the process going
- Track, analyze, improve, and share

In the seventh chapter, we detailed how you can create a SMarketing culture:

- Arrange for common training programmes, which should include the following:
  - o Tell them the story of why
  - o Make the story simple
  - o Help them create value
  - o Tell them how they can close the gaps
  - o Teach them to speak the same language
  - o Enable them to walk the talk
  - o Lay out the connection between activity and results
  - o Make them celebrate together
  - o Ensure that they are accountable

The next part was about what the size and elements of the team should be like.

- One-on-one team coordination
- Domain or area-wise division
- Independent Sales and Marketing team

We anticipate that SMarketing will definitely have bottlenecks as it is a new and radical way of thinking. We gave some guidelines on how to overcome bottlenecks:

- Budget for the best fit
- Update customer profile and persona
- Plot your customer's buyer journey with care
- List out what makes you different
- Focus on the marketing collateral
- Improve your website and online assets
- Evaluate and formalize your sales process

- Write down the SMarketing strategy
- Keep track of the progress and plan tactics

SMarketing is a new way of thinking that will enable you to change the way you approach Sales and Marketing. No matter what the hurdles may be, you will find that once you implement SMarketing and make it part of your DNA, you will find that it is a self-sustaining concept that will keep bringing sales at an astonishing speed.